D1799443

# in search of
# WELSHNESS

# Dedicated to Welsh exiles everywhere

*With thanks to my interview subjects:*
*Alan Rees, Richard Williams, David Davies, David Daniel,*
*Tony Fielden, Nerys Fielden, Clare Parry and Heinke Pulhorn.*

*Also to Alan, Dai Daniel, Tony, Graham Jones*
*and Dawn Greenall for their encouragement and help,*

*To Eifion Jenkins, editor, and Lefi Gruffudd of Y Lolfa*
*for their advice and support*

*And to my wife and family for their patience*

# in search of
# WELSHNESS

*Recollections and Reflections
of London Welsh exiles*

# Peter Daniels

First impression: 2011

© Copyright Peter Daniels and Y Lolfa Cyf., 2011

The contents of this book are subject to copyright, and may
not be reproduced by any means, mechanical or electronic,
without the prior, written consent of the publishers.

Editor: Eifion Jenkins

Cover design: Y Lolfa

ISBN: 978 184771 362 9

FSC
Published and printed in Wales
on paper from well maintained forests
by Y Lolfa Cyf., Talybont, Ceredigion SY24 5HE
*website* www.ylolfa.com
*e-mail* ylolfa@ylolfa.com
*tel* 01970 832 304
*fax* 832 782

# Contents

# Acknowledgements

I am greatly indebted to the following authors for permission to incorporate quotes from their named works in my book. The eloquence of the material has greatly enhanced the ability of this book to convey my search for Welshness.

Trevor Fishlock, *Wales and the Welsh* (London and Southampton, 1972).

Jan Morris, *Wales: Epic Views of a Small Country* (Oxford, 1985).

Pamela Petro, *Travels in an Old Tongue* (London, 1997).

Alun Richards, *Carwyn* (London, 1984).

Ned Thomas, *The Welsh Extremist* (London, 1971).

John Winterson Richards, extracts on pages 24, 25, 27 (x2), 32, 64 (x2), 65, 86, 87, 117 taken from *Xenophobe's® Guide to The Welsh* (London, 1993)

by permission of the publisher, Oval Books, London. www.xenophobes.com

J Geraint Jenkins, 'Life and Traditions in Rural Wales', World Conference on Records, 1980.

George Monbiot, various articles in *The Guardian*.

I have also drawn from the following works of reference:

John Davies, *A History of Wales* (London, 1993).

John Davies et al., *The Welsh Academy Encyclopaedia of Wales* (Cardiff, 2008).

Gwynfor Evans, *The Fight for Welsh Freedom* (Talybont, 2000).

John Humphries, *Freedom Fighters: Wales's Forgotten 'War', 1963–1993* (Cardiff, 2008).

Alun Richards, *Touch of Glory: 100 Years of Welsh Rugby* (London, 1980).

Various articles by Clive Betts from 'Cambria Politico: The Political Blog'.

Various IWA articles by John Osmond and Jon Gower.

An article from *The Guardian* by Marcel Theroux.

The words of American psychologist Carl Rogers.

The words of Professor T J Morgan, Swansea University.

# Illustrations

* Stradey Park, Llanelli, 1957 (© Tempest Collection, National Museum Wales)
* Old Castle Works, Llanelli, 1958 (© Crown copyright RCAHMW: Dylan Roberts)
* The North Dock, Llanelli's swimming pool (© Crown copyright RCAHMW: Dylan Roberts)
* Dai Losin's football team: Coronation Day Street Parade, 1953
* Old Deer Park (with thanks to Dave Jackson, chief photographer, London Welsh RFC)
* Huwie Barrington
* Dai 'Heart Attack' leading Ken Barrington and Gomer in the bowls club singing
* The author, Alan Rees, Alan Cole and 'Third Verse' Jenkins in full voice
* The 'deacons' in Cardiff for the cup
  (Thanks to Mike Howells and Lyn Hourahine for various bowls club photographs)
* Supporting Scarlets at London Irish (with thanks to Ian Williams and 'Stradegirl')
* Mam and Dad in Bournemouth
* With daughter Emma on my 50th
* With wife Gill, son Gareth and his wife Livvy, on my 60th
* Five budding England supporters: the grandchildren
* Alan Rees's birthday surprise (from Côr Meibion Dyffryn Aman's magazine)
* The president singing with his choir
* Level 3 Welsh learners performing a *cydadrodd* (group recitation)
* *Cylch Siarad* (Welsh speakers circle) in the London Welsh Centre bar
  (Two photographs courtesy of the London Welsh Association Magazine.)
* Tony Fielden supporting Radlett Cricket Club
* Nerys Fielden with Radlett's cricketing wives
  (Thanks for both photographs to Dick Scott and Colin Mansell of Radlett Cricket Club)
* Clare Parry
* Heinke Pulhorn on the Gower

# Introduction

THE WELSH LIKE to talk a lot. The Welsh like to talk a lot about themselves. They have this desperate need to tell the world that they are Welsh, as otherwise they are assumed to be English.

I too have felt this need to announce and explore my Welshness, to unburden myself of a 50-year-old chip on my shoulder.

I hate the fact that when asked where I live, I have often meekly stated that I come from Hertfordshire, near London, conditioned to believe that to say I'm not actually English but originally from Wales is a pedantic embellishment of no interest to the questioner.

I want really to identify myself as Welsh, so feel guilty that I cannot speak Welsh, a valuable and crucial means of differentiation, and that I have only recently in retirement become a Welsh learner.

I am constantly annoyed, boring my wife in the process, that the so-called British media choose to ignore the existence of our Principality, that there is little Welsh media, even in Wales itself, and that to watch BBC Wales or S4C in England, I have had to become a Sky subscriber.

My book sets out to chronicle the difficulties I have encountered both as a child in Wales, and as an adult in London, in hanging on to my Welshness.

It also explores the qualities that make the Welsh different from the English, and attempts to prove that there are values embodied in being Welsh which are actually worth preserving. It highlights our humanity and radicalism, our friendliness and sense of fun. So, despite the chip on my shoulder, the result is hopefully a humorous and human book.

At least my family and friends, for whom the book was

originally intended, all seemed to enjoy its first drafts. Friend Graham said, 'Why not publish?', and Dai Daniel from Welsh Learners said, 'I think the idea has legs'. But Graham's daughter Dawn, who works in publishing, said, 'It's too short'. Thus, as an experienced market research consultant, well used to interviewing all segments of the public and industry, I decided to add short biographies of other Welsh exiles and learners to my story, to explore whether their views were similar to mine, and whether my image of the Welsh as friendly and caring wasn't just seeing them through rose-tinted glasses.

I wanted also to investigate how their experiences were affected by coming from different backgrounds: from a first language Welsh-speaking family, from north and mid Wales rather than the south, from being first generation Welsh brought up in London as opposed to first generation English brought up in Wales, or coming from more recent generations brought up in an environment where the Welsh language has now achieved greater acceptance. Plus, I have spoken to a Welsh learner who wanted to learn Welsh despite being raised in England with an English mother and a Welsh, but non-Welsh-speaking, father, and even to total foreigners who have fallen so in love with Wales that they have also been motivated to learn the language.

The oldest Welsh exile I have written about is 80-year-old Alan Rees, a Welsh-speaking Welshman (*Cymro Cymraeg*) who hails from the Amman Valley, once a hotbed of both socialism and nonconformist religion, and a major centre of working class Welsh-language culture. His father was imprisoned both as a conscientious objector in the First World War and as a striking miner in the 1920s. Welsh was the language of the household and local working class culture but not considered relevant to government, business, or for getting on in the world. And the cause of Welsh nationalism was subservient to the greater worldwide struggle being undertaken in the name of socialism.

My own 1950s childhood in slightly more urbanised Llanelli

was far more anglicised. Welsh was the language of the outlying villages, but English was the language of the town centre. In a huge Labour stronghold, my father was a Conservative voter with a strong sense of Britishness in the aftermath of the Second World War. Unlike Alan Rees's family, we did listen to the Queen's Speech every Christmas Day.

Llanelli was the site of the very first Welsh-language primary school, but Welsh was still not then a compulsory subject after the third year of secondary school. And the newspapers, plus the new medium of television, were controlled from London, entirely in the English language.

The second half of my story focuses on my adult years in London, where Wales is almost invisible to both media and society, and how I have preserved my Welshness through the Welsh social scene in London, at Old Deer Park, home of London Welsh RFC, in the pubs and the chapels, and in the choir practices and Welsh classes of the London Welsh Centre in Gray's Inn Road in London's King's Cross.

Richard Williams, a fellow Welsh learner, has painted for me a similar picture of his childhood in 1960s rural Anglesey in north Wales, with a distinct division in his home district between the pupils of the separate English and Welsh language schools, and a father who believed that getting on in life meant an English-oriented education and getting out of the area.

Rural north Wales was badly affected by the 1930s Depression and another Welsh learner, David (Dafydd) Davies, was born in Essex after his Welsh father came to London in search of work because the family's tenant farm on the Llŷn peninsula was providing insufficient livelihood for himself, his parents and his three brothers. Welsh was the only language of the household, and Dafydd's father arrived in London a monoglot Welsh speaker.

I have then compared the contrasting stories of Dai Daniel, London-born of Glanaman parents, and Tony Fielden, first generation English, brought up in Colwyn Bay.

Dai's story is a perfect illustration of how the London

Welsh chapels once provided an essential support group for those wishing to preserve their Welshness, and their language, in exile. Dai speaks fluent Welsh, albeit with a north London accent. And despite living in London, he has immersed himself in the politics and history of the major efforts of the small vocal minority of Welshmen who achieved so much through the twentieth century to enhance the status of Welsh. It is a sad reflection of the limited attention given to Wales in the media that I was not aware of much of this political history highlighted for me by Dai, and I have therefore devoted two chapters of the book to it as an important component of my search for Welshness. In so doing, I have quoted extensively from key writings of the period, particularly Trevor Fishlock, Ned Thomas and, latterly, the Institute of Welsh Affairs.

Tony Fielden, a neighbour of mine in Radlett, Hertfordshire, was born in Colwyn Bay of English parents. He feels as Welsh as Dai, having fallen in love with the Welsh countryside, identified with the friendliness of the Welsh people, and with the emphasis placed on education and family values in contrast to the greater materialism he believes persists in England.

His daughter-in-law, Nerys, growing up in Newtown in mid Wales in the 1980s, in contrast to my 1950s Llanelli, benefited from the growing awareness and official acceptance of Welsh in the latter part of the twentieth century, receiving her education from Welsh-language schools, even sitting her A levels in Welsh.

She is now however enjoying married life with Tony's son in Radlett and is faced with the dilemma of how to pass on her Welshness to her children in exile, both in terms of values and language.

Ironically, as the status of Welsh has risen within its own borders, it has declined in exile. The major support group that was the multiplicity of Welsh chapels has substantially diminished, as religion has become less relevant to successive generations. There is one Welsh-language primary school in the whole of London, a good 45 minutes away from Nerys's family in Radlett. The 'national' media have become even more English-focused, and the so-called Welsh channels can only be viewed on Sky as opposed to terrestrial or even cable television. The one remaining feature that characterises Welshness is support for the Welsh rugby team, and that has become somewhat of a burden over the last few decades.

And all the exiles quoted in this book have been united in their desire to ensure that the preservation of their Welshness doesn't harm the prospects of their offspring from succeeding in the everyday environment in which they find themselves. There is no ghetto mentality among the Welsh.

However, the London Welsh Centre in Gray's Inn Road, while struggling financially, has thriving choirs and Welsh-language classes, and there is evidence from my Welsh Learners' Group that among both non-Welsh-speaking exiles and first generation Welsh, there is an increasing desire to learn Welsh to connect with their roots. Speaking Welsh is now much more the 'in' thing. One such learner is Clare, a 27-year-old barrister, brought up in north Staffordshire with an Essex mother and a Welsh, but non-Welsh-speaking, father.

And finally there is Heinke, a German girl, who was so taken by the friendliness and caring nature of the Welsh during her stay as a registrar in Morriston Hospital, that she has adopted the country as a second home, speaks fluent Welsh with a west Wales accent, and has even become a Scarlets season ticket holder.

What is it about the Welsh? Talkative. Friendly and caring, nurtured by a latent hypochondria. Lovers of learning, music and rugby. One-time religious, reflected in their need to be respectable despite a natural tendency for over-indulgence. A masculine-oriented society dominated by women. Lazy, but obsessively active when it's something they really believe in. Vocal and politically radical, except when it comes to their own independence, and a love of committees which tends to negate positive action on anything.

Strip away the language, the radicalism, the religion, the

rugby, one is still left with the feeling that the Welsh have an innate desire to be friendly and helpful, to be one's equal and not one's superior or inferior. And if that is all we pass on to our offspring and future generations, then it will be well worth the effort.

But why not perpetuate the language, support the rugby team, and gain more than a measure of independence while we are at it?

# An autobiography

## Welsh Peter

# 1

# A Scarlet till I die

THE WORLD IS unaware of Wales.

This is particularly true of Americans. The driver of our Hollywood tour bus wanted to know our nationalities. He offered up the usual suspects, then said 'Any others?' One voice said: 'Germany'. I said: 'Wales'. He laughed: 'That's a new one; where's that? Isn't it somewhere up by Scotland?' An Englishman roared with delight.

We passed an apartment block owned by Anthony Hopkins. I failed to take the opportunity to declare his Welshness. We then discovered that the driver had a passion for golf. So on leaving the bus I suggested he look up the venue for the 2010 Ryder Cup. Perhaps I should also have mentioned Ian Woosnam, a Welsh winner of the US Masters. Or even a fact, gleaned from a xenophobic Welsh website, that four of the first six USA presidents were actually of Welsh descent.

The Welsh seem always to believe that there is a Welsh identity hidden behind every celebrity. It has been claimed that America itself was named after Richard Amerik (Ap Meurig), a native of Glamorgan, who became a wealthy collector of customs in Bristol and acted as an intermediary between Henry VII and John Cabot as the latter explored the eastern coastline of the New World.

Yet Americans are still unaware of Wales, and the rest of the UK is also probably not that aware of Llanelli (population 44,000), Carmarthenshire, south Wales. And the non-rugby followers of this world may not even be aware of the Scarlets, the town's rugby club, now redefined as a Welsh rugby region in the Magners (soon to be RoboDirect Pro 12) League with a mandate to maintain the development of the game in west and north Wales.

The Scarlets are Llanelli's pride and joy. The population believes that the team and Stradey Park are known the whole world over for a famous 1972 victory over the touring New Zealand All Blacks and for an equally famous victory over the then world champions, Australia, in 1993; and further known as the 12 times winners and 17 times finalists of the Welsh Challenge Cup in its 30-year tenure as a major competition; and more recently for reaching three Heineken European Cup semi-finals, to be denied dramatically and famously on two occasions by late penalties, in one instance via an upright and a crossbar.

I hail from Llanelli, but first, and foremost, I am a Scarlet.

I was raised on a diet of pronouncements by my father about heroes past, especially Albert Jenkins, legendary centre three-quarter of the 1920s, who never quite performed for Wales in the manner in which he mesmerised Stradey's 'Tanner Bank'. My father gave me a scarlet jersey on my 10th Christmas, assuring me it was once worn by the great man himself. Of such tender years, and with no logos on jerseys in those days, who was I to question such an assertion, even if it was 30 years since Albert Jenkins had last played?

The owner of the small grocery shop opposite our house was Ewart Thomas, famous as the Scarlets' full-back against the touring New South Wales Waratahs in 1927, who was forced to leave the field injured with 10 minutes to play, allowing the Waratahs to turn around a deficit and win the game.

The steelworker I said hello to every morning on route to school was not just any old steelworker. He was Griff Bevan, of Llanelli, the Royal Navy, and once capped for Wales at prop in the late 1940s.

Every Saturday afternoon I walked down the railway line

to Stradey Park, initially sitting on my father's knee in the grandstand, subsequently sitting with the mass of other kids on the little wall that separated the pitch from the Tanner Bank, to then run on to the pitch itself at half time to collect autographs, interrupting the players as they ate their oranges. The lasting memory of Stradey is of hordes of kids charging on at half-time, disrupting the players grouped together for their break. No dressing room lectures from the coaches in those far-gone amateur days.

If I wasn't supporting Llanelli, I was supporting the Welsh national side. It is difficult to put into words the significance of rugby to the Welsh nation. With a population of only three million, it is comprehensively dwarfed by its 50 million-plus English neighbours, politically, culturally and economically. Therefore when it actually finds a territory, in this case a sport, in which it has competed on equal terms for over a century, this inevitably has to become a focus of attention.

Welsh nationalists, such as Gwynfor Evans, have argued lucidly that a Welsh identity, in the absence of any political or military clout, has survived through the centuries largely as a result of the preservation of the Welsh language and its use as the medium of communication in the nonconformist church. I buy into this, and my attempt to relearn the Welsh language is evidence of my support. But in childhood, Wales for me was identified through its rugby.

My friends and I walked with pride when the Scarlets had six players in the Welsh team to play the Australians in 1958. One of those players, Carwyn James, the late, great fly half, and later coach to the successful 1971 British Lions in New Zealand, once stood as a parliamentary candidate for Plaid Cymru. He won 8,000 votes, which by coincidence just happened to be the average home gate at Stradey.

Llanelli though, even apart from its rugby club, is a proud town. Not a pretty town, it once boasted a promenade of steelworks, now thankfully replaced by the attractive national coastal path, and the Nicklaus-designed Machynys Peninsula

Golf and Country Club with its wonderful views of Gower. It is an industrial town, but one surrounded by the beautiful, rolling hills of rural Carmarthenshire.

Geographically separated by the Loughor Bridge from Glamorgan and the bulk of what was once the prosperous south Wales coalfield, it is also not pre-eminent in Carmarthenshire, being now governed from the county town of Carmarthen. It is also bypassed by the main trunk road from Swansea to Carmarthen, now partly the M4. In fact it is a sort of lay-by.

But this splendid isolation has created an exclusivity, a uniqueness. It is not part of a rambling ribbon development typical of much of the Glamorgan and Gwent valleys, where one village merges imperceptibly into the next. It is very much its own land. If you are from the area, you are definitely 'a Llanelli boy'.

It is also home to the last major rugby outpost before the west coast of Wales, and as such serves as a sporting focus for the whole of south-west Wales. With rugby far more important than politics, Llanelli people believe that Llanelli and not the administrative centre of Carmarthen is the emotional capital of Carmarthenshire. And the new rugby region of Llanelli Scarlets (now shortened to Scarlets) services in addition the needs and ambitions of the rugby folk of mid and north Wales.

The Carmarthenshire valleys and hills surrounding Llanelli are actually the site of Max Boyce's mythical 'Outside Half Factory', with Barry John, Carwyn James, Gareth Davies and Jonathan Davies all born within a five-mile radius of each other, and Phil Bennett not far away in the Llanelli suburb of Felinfoel.

Unlike industrial Glamorgan and Gwent, with their closeness to England, and their large-scale English immigration of the nineteenth and early twentieth centuries, Llanelli was also 50 per cent Welsh speaking, although it has to be said that the Welsh language being spoken in the town on market days hailed largely from the agricultural hills and valleys surrounding the town, rather than from the townspeople themselves.

But to be from Llanelli was to be Welsh. The town even possesses its own Welsh anthem, 'Sosban Fach', whose derivation I presume is linked to the town's industrial concentration on steel and tinplate. The song was played on the Stradey public address system to announce the scoring of a Scarlet penalty goal, and we have also inherited 'Yma o Hyd' [Still here], Dafydd Iwan's protest anthem about the preservation of the Welsh language, which heralds every Scarlet try.

My mother once chased a local scallywag down the road after he had knocked on our front door and done a runner: a very common local pastime. 'Come here you cheeky Arab,' she cried. 'I'm not a cheeky Arab,' the kid replied, 'I'm a bloody Welshman.'

However, there must have been some immigration, for Swansea folk refer to us as 'Turks'. Theories abound as to the origins of this nickname, but an Iranian friend of mine, to whom I had casually divulged this information, once enthusiastically accosted me in Ikea while shopping, to announce that he had discovered on good authority that the Llanelli population was so-called because the Turks who had landed in Swansea docks turned left for Llanelli rather than right for Glamorgan along with the other immigrants.

There are boundless childhood memories of Italian cafés and ice cream, German and Polish miners, Jewish shopkeepers, even a Lithuanian Jew named Michael Howard (former leader of the Conservative Party); but unfortunately no Turks.

Llanelli however has taken to the name, and I recall seeing Turkish flags being brandished by the Stradey Park faithful in support of their beloved Scarlets.

In return, Llanelli call Swansea people 'Jacks'. This is not, as it might at first seem, because of any association with sailors. The name in fact derives from a dog, Swansea Jack, who rescued a drowning man in Swansea Bay.

When in South Africa for the 1997 British Lions rugby tour, my wife and I were introduced in the bar, on our first evening, to the other members of our party. A Swansea man was 'in the chair' and he grudgingly added my wife and me to his order, protesting that he had 'come 5,000 f***ing miles just to buy a Turk a drink!'

Such tribalism is often seen as more important than Wales itself and must, I sense, have been a contributory factor to the one-time Big Five Welsh rugby selectors' frequent inability to agree on a team that could successfully perform as a coherent whole, or even to the continued belief of Welshmen that they are incapable of governing themselves.

Ironically, however, in the 1940s, you could live in Llanelli, but you could not be born or cremated there. Births took place across the Loughor Bridge in Gorseinon Hospital (a place of birth I share with that well-known Lithuanian Jew), and the first crematorium to be built in the 1950s was 50 miles away in Pontypridd. A closer one was subsequently opened in Morriston, Swansea, now overlooked by the DVLA offices, but only in 2005 did Llanelli finally possess a crematorium of its own.

My passport thus declares my place of birth to be Llwchwr (the Welsh for Loughor). This spelling is pleasing to my Welsh pride, as the lack of English vowels I imagine must confuse foreign customs officials. However, on recently crossing the Loughor Bridge into the village, I encountered a sign announcing that I had now entered the newly-created County Borough of Swansea. 'Oh my God!' I screamed, 'I'm a bloody Jack!'

PS: Stradey Park has now been demolished and replaced by a 15,000-seater, state-of-the-art, new stadium named Parc y Scarlets.

# 2

# Welsh or British?

THE REGULARS AT the Red Lion in Radlett, Hertfordshire, know me as 'Welsh Peter', but I spent my childhood not knowing whether I was Welsh or British, or even English.

My father, Bill Daniels, a fluent Welsh speaker, was of long-standing farming stock from the area around Llanarthney in the Towy valley above Carmarthen – an area of such rich farmland that it is known as *Gelli Aur* (Golden Grove).

His father, Tom Daniels, owned a stable of shire horses, and during the Second World War his horses and carts both collected Llanelli's refuse and delivered Buckley's beer and coal around the town. After the war he managed the Old Castle Inn for the brewery. The pub sat alongside the railway line bringing coal down from the mine at Cynheidre; the same line that ran past Stradey Park. On the other side of the line stood the Llanelli steelworks, where my father worked as a shipping clerk, later as a sales manager.

Dad often helped behind the Old Castle bar, especially on Thursday lunchtime, when the shift workers got paid, only to spend most of their wages lubricating their throats after the heat of eight hours over the furnaces.

As a young boy, I was a frequent visitor to my grandparents' pub, and I still refer to a pub's closing time as 'stop tap', an analogy borrowed from the shutting down of the steel furnaces. The pub regulars always had a welcoming word for me, especially Edgar Staples, a retired steelworker and permanent occupant of his reserved seat at the end of the bar. Edgar also spent a lot of time on his allotment which I visited most Sundays to collect a sprig of mint for my mother's roast lamb. Edgar reared chickens, and at one time became distraught over their continued failure to produce any eggs. Another pub regular, Jack Maggie (his wife's name was Margaret) decided to creep into the allotment at the dead of night and place some eggs underneath the chickens. Next morning Edgar was overjoyed until he realised these particular eggs had already been hard boiled.

After my grandfather died, my grandmother continued to run the pub with the help of my Aunty Etta. My 'Gramma', a little woman, still had no problem dealing with the tough steelworkers, as her regulars would soon sort out any problematic customer for her.

In the current age of gang warfare, drugs, shootings and muggings, it seems strange to recall these hardened steelworkers as warm-hearted, friendly characters. After all, they and the miners formed the physical backbone of many a Welsh forward pack, and the demise of both the mining and the steel industries is partly behind the decline in Welsh rugby fortunes.

Yes there were fights, especially between Neath and Llanelli supporters on the excursion trains laid on for internationals at the Arms Park. I recall one such journey when the communication cord was pulled a dozen or more times. But for the most part, these were fights of fists, not guns and knives.

Yet one wouldn't describe our local neighbourhood as particularly soft. Witnessing two rival gangs of kids throwing stones and cans at each other down our back lane, I once came within a millimetre of losing an eye as a flattened tin can found my face. With blood gushing out of what appeared to be my eye socket, my parents must have thought the worse.

I have heard it reported that nowadays Llanelli, like many other small towns, has a drug culture. And the centre of activity is Station Road, a long mundane street of pubs and kebab houses, rather than shops, which links the station to the town centre. Talking to the priest before my mother's funeral, he complained that the walk down Station Road to his church was fraught with danger, and that every street in the parish had at least one family in which drugs were a problem.

However, visiting Llanelli during the 1999 Rugby World Cup with friend Keith and son Gareth in tow, I ventured forth into one of these Station Road hostelries, and rather than a den of iniquity, I found it full of many of my old school friends. It was more 'grab a granny' than hip-hop and drugs.

After 40 years in north London and Hertfordshire, I am no longer qualified to judge the truth about Welsh everyday life, but I do know that the annual golf holiday undertaken with a group of mixed friends from Essex, which has taken in Ireland, Scotland, France, Cornwall, Portugal and Spain over recent years, encountered the friendliest welcome of all in Wales. To my own surprise, the hospitality even rivalled Ireland.

John Winterson Richards points out in his *Xenophobe's Guide to the Welsh* that there is a quite distinctive Welsh tradition of hospitality: 'In Welsh history the guest was sacred. Once welcomed to the hearth, whether by a prince or pauper, the visitor, even if a perfect stranger, could expect the very best the household had to offer, and would be treated literally as one of the family.'

On our arrival at Morriston Golf Club in the drizzling rain, my Essex friends and I were ushered into the clubhouse by the pro, Darryl Rees, offered coffee, and told to relax until the rain had eased – no pressure about tee times. And on watching my abysmal performance as I later came down the 18th, Darryl told me to grab my six iron and took me back to the practice field for a free impromptu lesson. 'No Llanelli boy is going to play golf as badly as that!' he declared.

Darryl's hospitality has since been extended to Hollywood's Michael Douglas while Mr Douglas was visiting his in-laws in Mumbles.

My Essex friends had earlier been surprised to hear

Darryl giving a golf lesson to a group of local youngsters through the medium of Welsh. The English always assume that the language is only spoken in the deepest crevices of Snowdonia, but it is equally alive and well in the Swansea Valley as well as Carmarthenshire.

Also on our golf tour of south Wales, at Carmarthen Golf Club, I came upon an old London client, Cledwyn Davies. Cledwyn had previously worked in London for the Post Office, before moving to Cardiff as its marketing manager for Wales. (A very useful hospitality contact in the 1980s for internationals at the old Arms Park.) He and his family then bought a sub-post office in Llangain, outside Carmarthen; a 24/7 job if ever there was one.

From the bar of the Carmarthen Golf Club high on a hill, he proudly pointed out his village down below, and spoke glowingly of the lifestyle: the scenery, his relaxed if busy existence, the friendly people, 'the lowest crime rate in the country', with culture only an hour away in Cardiff if you wanted it. I was envious.

My wife claims that I'm much happier when on holiday in Wales. Trips 'home' have always been filled with laughter, usually in the pub or standing on the Tanner Bank. I recall, on one such occasion, a Stradey Park wit responding to a piece of foul play, telling the famous Barbarians rugby team to 'Go home to Barbaria'.

Life in Wales, with its socialistic and liberal traditions, was about being part of a community and not about making a quick buck. Education was placed above wealth in the social hierarchy. Welsh millionaires were few and far between, and it was grammar school teachers who were considered the pillars of society, and a dustman was to be admired if he was in possession of a university degree.

The downside of this tendency is that we almost discourage ambition and are innately suspicious of anyone with wealth or power, especially our own Welsh politicians.

John Winterson Richards writes in his *Xenophobe's Guide*

*to the Welsh* that the Welsh are 'generally fond of eccentrics. The unforgivable eccentricity is to be successful... it is considered almost bad form to better one's lot in life.'

John goes on to say that the Welsh have no interest in commerce or success, yet they enjoy doing business, the talk and haggling, the social side, and a fascination with technology. And being stubborn and bloody-minded, they are capable of extraordinary opportunism, everywhere in the world, except in Wales.

According to Alun Richards in *Touch of Glory: 100 years of Welsh Rugby*, 'we breed critics like mayfly in permanent hatch' and 'very often ambition is a risqué word. "Watch it, boy," the very terraced houses seem to be saying at times, or, "Who do you think you are?"'

The upside is that we also have a great love of deflating pomposity. I recall anyone showing any snobbish upper class tendencies, often announced by the possession of a double barrelled surname, being quickly put in his place. The lovely sounding derogatory Welsh word *crach* or *crachach* was used to describe such people.

Welsh travel writer, Jan Morris, states in her book *Wales: Epic Views of a Small Country* that, 'It was not simply romanticising to claim, even in 1997, that in many parts of Wales a particular kind of society still flourished in a way generally forgotten elsewhere. A relationship almost familial, still bound friends, neighbours and even opponents. Class meant far less than it did in England, and sect had become almost irrelevant.'

These thoughts were echoed by George Monbiot, an English author now residing in Wales, who commented in a *Guardian* article that observations over two years of walking through the valleys and over the hills, had led him 'to form the impression that Wales is less socially stratified, less grasping, more liberal than the rest of Britain'.

The other major facet of Welsh life, which may also have contributed to this desire to promote the common good over individual success, was religion, with the nonconformist chapels and not the Church of England as its focus. There were two main offshoots of this. One was an innate conservatism, sometimes bordering on narrow-mindedness. John Winterson Richards writes that there is 'conflict between respectability and a natural indulgence... tolerated as long as it doesn't cause a public scandal'.

American writer, Pamela Petro, in her book *Travels in an Old Tongue* in which she relives her journey around the globe in search of Welsh speakers, feels she encountered a similar Welshness in, of all places, 'the swank city of Buenos Aires... This was the Wales of chapels, of temptations forsaken, of temperance and tea parties, of musical harmonies baited to catch the ear of an austere, Welsh-speaking God.'

In the mid-1990s, Pamela believed this to be a throwback to 'the Wales of the last century'. I can tell her it was alive and well in 1950s Llanelli.

Other, more positive, qualities emanating from this religious focus were a tradition of honesty (Taffy wasn't a thief) and politeness. I recall my father, ever the gentleman, always doffing his hat to every passing lady, and again standing when a lady entered the room. I, in turn, was taught always to respect the wisdom of my elders. Again quoting John Winterson Richards: 'the Welsh have a traditional respect for the idea of the village or chapel elder, who develops a sort of dignity not out of place in a High Court judge.'

The other major aspect of chapel-going was hymn singing. Congregations even gathered regularly at the *cymanfa ganu*, particularly on bank holidays, purely to sing hymns. To hell with the prayers!

Wales has always had a strong musical and poetry tradition over the centuries, but the singing of the 19th and 20th centuries emanated from the nonconformist religions, with the early years of the 20th century witnessing several major religious revivals. Many of the chapels have sadly now disappeared, but the male voice choirs are still blasting out 'Cwm Rhondda'.

I recall taking my mother to a local pub for Sunday lunch, to be sat next to a large farming family gathering, who burst into song, usually a hymn, in between every food course.

And when my wife and I recently attended a St David's Day dinner dance sponsored by the London Welsh Rugby Supporters Club, my wife, who hails from Essex, observed that this was the first time that she had attended a formal dinner dance function when the dancing was preceded by hymn singing over the coffee.

My father's family were Welsh Methodists worshipping at Tabernacle. They weren't, however, regular chapelgoers. This was the era of Sunday closing, and they valued their day of rest from the pub. It was also an opportunity for me to have Sunday lunch in my grandmother's kitchen alongside the Aga and the countless horse brasses. I remember my grandfather as a strict, serious man, but perhaps that was because of the Sunday morning I locked him in the cellar while he was cleaning the beer pipes.

My father first met my mother in the offices of the Llanelly Steel Co., a stone's throw from the pub. As a result of this meeting, his, and thus my, anglicisation began.

Mam was from Seaside, a tough working class area set amongst Llanelli's docks and steelworks. But she clearly rose above it. She once told me that in her younger years she was known locally as 'the duchess'.

Her family hailed from south Pembrokeshire, 'little England beyond Wales', settled by Scandinavians, Flemish and Normans prior to 1066 and all that. They were thus non-Welsh-speaking. There is an imaginary language border, known as the Landsker line, that cuts through the heart of Pembrokeshire, dividing Welsh from English-derived place names. Apparently the peoples on either side of this line mixed little across several centuries in the Middle Ages, preserving their separate languages and culture.

My mother's family were also not chapel. They attended a little Anglican church in Seaside called St John's, moving later to the lower Llanelli parish's largest church of St Peter's. The parish was part of the Church *in* Wales, as opposed to the more commonly assumed description 'Church *of* England'. The Anglican Church in Wales is not the church of the establishment, as in England, and it has always amazed me how Welsh-minded politicians in 1920 actually succeeded in disestablishing the church, given the centuries of pressure put on the Welsh by Westminster to abandon their culture and traditions.

My father was persuaded to 'switch codes', and later became a church warden of St Peter's. I attended Sunday school, and was also encouraged, without success, to join the choir. Despite a love of hymn singing, I have always found Anglican hymns insipid in comparison to Methodist, and also harboured a dislike of church as opposed to chapel singing, pitched as it seemed for sopranos. Add to this a tone deaf choirmaster and an innate teenager's shyness, and the church choir was not for me.

Church did however have one advantage over chapel: a much more active youth club, providing far greater contact with the opposite sex. That is, as long as you showed your face at Sunday morning communion. Otherwise presence was barred from the club on Sunday night.

The social event of the year was the Whit Tuesday excursion to Tenby or Barry Island, when a whole Great Western train was hired for the day to transport all the Sunday schools of the town en masse to the seaside.

In those days trains did not consist of open carriages but a corridor running past separate compartments, each with its own door and window blinds: a paradise for pubescent teenagers wanting a kiss, cuddle or even a grope.

Despite a church, as opposed to a chapel upbringing, Welsh hymns were not lost to me. Their permanent presence in school assembly, and later rugby, pub and university evenings in Aberystwyth, meant that I put to memory the words of some two dozen Welsh hymns, despite not speaking Welsh nor understanding any of the words I was singing.

The daily school assembly always incorporated a hymn in Welsh, and on Thursdays, a visit from a local chapel preacher, who would deliver a 20-minute sermon in Welsh, completely oblivious to the fact that half his audience couldn't understand a word that he was saying. Even the school song was sung in Welsh, never to be translated for us monoglot English speakers.

University at Aberystwyth was also about music and singing in general, as well as Welsh hymn singing in particular. On Saturday evenings we had at our disposal a choice of half a dozen pubs, each with a different musical offering, ranging from jazz, folk singing, rock and roll, to Welsh hymns at the White Horse.

Then on Sunday evenings, singing would erupt again at coffee evenings organised at the different university hostels (usually female), when volume, tone and harmony would be achieved even without the assistance of alcohol.

Another major influence on the preservation of my Welshness was the presence in Llanelli of the 1962 Welsh National Eisteddfod, with the excitement generated by the male voice choral contests, and more proactively, the late-night, post-pub, hymn singing on the Town Hall steps. My other abiding memory of the Eisteddfod was of an old monoglot Welsh-speaking farmer relying on his grandson to translate any English words for him.

For the rest, my upbringing was British as opposed to Welsh-focused. My family were stout royalists. We first acquired a television to be able to watch the coronation of Queen Elizabeth II. The Last Night of the Proms, with 'Rule Britannia', 'Land of Hope and Glory' and 'Jerusalem', was a must-watch annual event. On Armistice Day, both my parents marched past the cenotaph, my mother with the British Red Cross and my father with the RAF Association.

And while all my friends took caravan holidays on Gower or in Tenby, we went 'upmarket' to the English south coast, even if it meant a 12-hour journey by coach, or should I say coaches, as there were usually four changes on route.

Each evening of the holiday was spent at the local repertory theatre, or at variety shows featuring many of the famous TV, usually English, performers of the day, followed by hours at the various stage doors collecting autographs.

In the early 20th century, Welsh society, for the most part, still looked to England. Even our local streets bore such names as Albert Street and Queen Victoria Road. Local streets are now given Welsh names such as *Waun Lan yr Afon*. Our Welsh identity has become politically more correct.

My father, in a Labour stronghold, was staunch Tory, chairman of the Conservative Club and even of the West Wales Association of Conservative Clubs. If the truth be known however, the Conservative Club was just a good place to have a drink, and rumour had it, unbeknown to my father, that 90 per cent of its members were probably Labour voters. I joined the Young Conservatives, along with Michael Howard, and even stood as a Conservative in mock school elections.

Dad believed that Wales was incapable of governing itself, but since leaving home my own politics have become more nationalistic and socialistic. In 1966, I was at the London party to welcome Gwynfor Evans as Plaid Cymru's first Westminster MP, albeit as an enthusiastic bystander.

Whatever career aspirations my father may have had were disrupted by the war, but he did have an innate desire to contribute to society. He was not only a church warden and Conservative Club chairman, but also a mason, and a grand master no less. Two representatives from each of these three organisations eventually carried the coffin at his funeral.

Dad never, however, attempted to force the masonic ritual down my throat. I was not a big fan of its formality, and I was surprised to learn, over a drink with a flag bearer of the bardic *Gorsedd* staying at our hotel during the 2000

National Eisteddfod, that there are strong links between the masonic movement and the bardic traditions of the National Eisteddfod.

But my appreciation of Welsh ritual and hymn singing is a different matter. I am usually close to tears singing the anthem at the Millennium Stadium. John Winterson Richards suggests that while Welsh manners are most of the time fairly informal, we have a great respect for, and love of, ceremony. It is the actor in us.

At the time of my father's funeral, the parish priest was an insipid little man and, unwittingly, I left the funeral arrangements solely in his hands. There were 200 at the crematorium. My father was a popular man. But I don't remember even one hymn being sung, certainly not in Welsh.

Years later, when visiting the book of remembrance in the crematorium chapel vestry, I heard a similar packed house, in the chapel next door, raising the roof with a classic Welsh hymn. I was filled with guilt, and ensured that at my mother's funeral Welsh hymns would be sung.

My parents, however, discouraged me from learning Welsh in school. After three years study I had to choose between Welsh, Latin or French for GCE. 'What use is Welsh to you?' my mother would say. 'Latin is essential; it is the foundation of all other languages.' So Latin and French it was.

This was despite our Welsh teacher awarding unheard of exam results above 90 per cent, when 50 per cent had previously been the norm, in an effort to encourage a band of his pupils to stay with the cause.

Sharing a flat in Finchley in the 1960s with several Welsh speakers, I would rue my decision. Incidentally, being Welsh, all my flatmates were teachers.

I did later, when first married, take Welsh lessons from the minister at Harrow Welsh Chapel, but time became too precious. So it is, 30 years later, in retirement, that I am now realising my long-held ambition to learn Welsh.

As a child, not only was learning Welsh discouraged, but

I was, in addition, sent by my mother to elocution classes to improve my English pronunciation. (There were also piano lessons: you will never lack friends at a party if you can play the piano.) Elocution was also a school subject taught on a part-time basis by the same teacher, the venerable Mrs Yvonne Watkin Rees. I have already warned you against those with double-barrelled surnames. To the boys however she was 'Maggie Soundbox'.

I achieved grade three in recitation, and competed in an eisteddfod in Ammanford, after being bribed with 2/6d. to conquer my shyness of going out on stage.

I also won a poetry reading prize at the school eisteddfod. Ironically the piece, which was called 'Old Morgan', required uttering Old Morgan's own words in a particularly pronounced Welsh accent. I beat Mike Hopkins's reading of Rudyard Kipling's 'If' into second place.

It is ironic that my mother, when visiting London in her later years, took great pride in her Welshness, and her ability to mouth a variety of Welsh phrases which her listeners were unable to understand.

My parents' Welshness was however more positively reflected in their belief in education. And from an early age it was never questioned that my schooling would extend other than to university.

The ultimate objective was learning and respect rather than wealth. Even when in full time employment, my parents were more impressed by my achieving managerial status in such major companies as Lever and H J Heinz than if I'd become a self-made millionaire.

What university did offer me however was a bridge to the 'real world' away from the apron strings. And leaving home after university meant London.

# 3

# The Mecca of London

I ENDED UP living in London partly by accident. An alternative interpretation would be that I was driven by economic necessity, with the English capital being the most likely fertile breeding ground for worthwhile employment.

Leaving University College of Wales, Aberystwyth, in June 1964, with joint honours in economics and international politics, I was courted by GKN, steelmakers of Corby, to join their systems analysis department. After visiting their plant, I was given the impression that my appointment was a fait accompli. Two months later, in October 1964, they reneged on the deal. By now I was desperate to take the first job opportunity that presented itself.

This happened to be with Tothill Press of Westminster, later to become National Trade Press based in Fleet Street, and eventually IPC Business Press.

It was a dead-end research assistant's position in an old-fashioned, not very dynamic organisation. Who else would advertise in *The Economist* for graduate staff? On the other hand, who else would bother to browse *The Economist* for such job advertisements?

I spent the next three years working at NTP Press while at the same time applying to all and sundry to gain alternative business employment, and I finally kick-started my career at Lever Brothers as an assistant market research manager.

I was asked in my interview why I wanted to join Lever. I gave the stock answer, praising them as a dynamic, competitive, successful organisation. The personnel manager replied: 'Then what's going to happen to this go-ahead organisation if you join us?' I will never understand to this day why they didn't offer the job to any number of marketing trainees that they already had on their books.

Two years invaluable experience at Lever, plus an Advertising Association Diploma acquired at night school, paved the way for a career in marketing, advertising and market research, which, for the most part, meant working and therefore living in London or south-east England.

I must confess in any case to being a bit star-struck by the bright lights of London, even from an early age – its sheer size, the historical buildings, the theatres, the Albert Hall, the sporting venues including Wembley, Wimbledon and Lords.

As a child, on FA Cup Final days, I would sit glued to the TV from early morning, soaking up every bit of atmosphere. And as a visiting teenager, even the complexities of the Underground held a weird fascination.

In those days Wales had far less to offer. Socially it was a strange mixture of masculine over-indulgence and a narrow-mindedness which disapproved of women drinking in pubs, let alone children, as is the norm in this day and age. Time at university seemed to be the only occasion when such social mores could be acceptably broken.

Cardiff did have the Arms Park, and my father first took me to a Wales v Ireland rugby international in 1955. He seemed to have the knack of acquiring international tickets at will. On this occasion he managed to get hold of five tickets for adjacent seats in the giant North Stand, and then persuaded the gate attendant to let me in as a sixth body to squeeze in among the five men.

This ability of my father to lay his hands on such priceless commodities meant that when debenture seats were introduced in the 1960s at £50 a seat, I showed no interest in them, little realising that they would increase in value to £5,000, and that tickets in the 1970s and onwards would become like gold dust. The Welsh Rugby Union now has a different policy, with debentures, currently valued at £5,000, having to be sold back at their original purchase price. In my old age I have acquired two such seats, representing my only bit of Welsh real estate since selling my mother's house after her death.

The Arms Park was my boyhood Mecca. The week after being taken by my father, I returned on a school trip to watch the Welsh Schoolboys take on South of Scotland, and I was able to point out the sights to my then less well-informed classmates.

Even in those days rugby excursions involved a routine which incorporated more than just the rugby, although at that age this meant food rather than alcohol. And as a mere 12-year-old the height of sophistication was represented by chicken and chips from Littlewood's self-service restaurant. By the Millennium this had been overtaken by a pork butty with crackling and apple sauce from a stall outside St David's Hall. However we have now progressed to the rather more opulent and expensive restaurants of Cardiff Bay.

In the 1950s, Cardiff only had the Arms Park. It had literally only just been designated the capital city. There was no Welsh Assembly, no Cardiff Bay, no St David's Hall, no Millennium Centre (Wales's answer to the Sydney Opera House), nor a Millennium Stadium. It did have the Welsh Folk Museum out at St Fagans, and Cardiff Castle, both of which I now really appreciate as an adult, but they were insufficient to attract a young 20-year-old. In any case, a Scarlets supporter couldn't live in Cardiff.

Also, in the 1950s, Wales was under the radar as far as popular British (or should I say English) media were concerned. I understand that the BBC originally had a Western rather than a separate Welsh regional service, and ITV only saw the birth of a shared commercial station, Television Wales and West, for south Wales, with north Wales kept separate as part of the Granada franchise designed mainly to service north-west England.

Gwynfor Evans, in his book *The Fight for Welsh Freedom*,

speaks of the years of effort involved in creating the Welsh-language TV channel S4C, and ironically adds that all we need now is a genuine English-language Welsh channel.

Even today BBC Wales offers little that is different from the normal BBC1 or BBC2 coverage, outside the 6 p.m. regional news and the occasional rugby match. And to watch such gems I have had to purchase Sky, as terrestrial TV in England fails to give me the option of watching BBC Wales or S4C. Wales is part of the UK, so I shouldn't have to live in Wales to access Welsh television.

The London 'quality' papers no longer have Welsh editions, and staying in Cowbridge in the Vale of Glamorgan after the 2007 Wales v Ireland game, *The Sunday Times* sports coverage could only talk of England's victory over Scotland, and the renaissance of a certain Jonny Wilkinson. In fact the five sports pages contained no less than seven photographs of the wonder boy.

Since the birth of the Guinness (now Aviva) Premiership in England, we have been lucky to get the scores of Magners League games, let alone any actual match reports.

You cannot buy Wales's 'national newspaper', the oddly named *Western Mail*, anywhere in London, including, I discovered recently, Paddington Station. On the other hand you can buy *The Irish Times* or *The New York Times* in abundance at any newsagent.

My final gripe, for I am now on my hobbyhorse, is the exclusion of all things Welsh from any representation of Britishness. I refuse to recognise the Union Jack flag as it lacks any Welsh reference. The English have also laid claim to the British national anthem, 'God Save the Queen', but to this they are welcome, if just for the direness of the music, irrespective of any views I may have on the appropriateness of the monarchy.

The ultimate ignominy is that not being a Welsh resident I am prevented under the present voting system from democratically voicing my discontent, although even voting in Wales is of little value with only 40 MPs (possibly soon to be reduced to 30) represented at Westminster. Pamela Petro describes Wales as 'the least democratic country in Europe'.

With the exception of the public banning of the Welsh language, the English used far less force than in Ireland to quell Welsh identity. What they did instead was to dismiss, or almost ignore it, as something trivial and inferior. In a strange way, this is more damning than the use of force. It has tended to divide the indigenous population rather than unite it. In my 1950s childhood, people aspired to be more English. If public office demanded a Welsh tongue, this was backward-looking and unfair to the non-Welsh-speaking majority.

Economically, England has always represented the dominant market and, in days gone by, cattle, sheep and milk all used to find their way to London. (As an aside, apparently the broad-rimmed hat of the Welsh drovers was the original forerunner of both the Texan stetson and the Mexican sombrero.) I was later to be grateful to the milk train for allowing me to leave Cardiff as late as 11 p.m. after an international rugby match, to arrive in Paddington at 6 p.m. on the Sunday morning just in time for the opening of the London Underground; not a schedule that current so-called service-conscious transport companies would dream of providing. These days, when 5 p.m. kick-offs are arranged to suit the needs of the TV companies, it is not possible to catch a train back to London after 7 p.m. at the end of the match.

The Welsh road and rail system, in any case, only runs eastwards towards England, and I recall going on a family holiday to Llandudno (as a one-off change from Bournemouth and Eastbourne), to find that the train route from south to north Wales was via Shrewsbury across the English border.

The English author, George Monbiot, quoted earlier, speaks in *The Guardian* of a recent impetus to provide Wales with a totally internal north-south railway link, describing 'the railway map of Wales' as 'a classic indicator of an extractive economy. The lines extend either towards London or towards the ports...

they are likely to have been built to empty the nation of its wealth for the benefit of another.'

Anyway, exposed through childhood to this economic and media bias, it is not surprising that my cultural focus gravitated towards London rather than south Wales. And in my first month in London, I saw Arsenal at Highbury, Spurs at White Hart Lane, Middlesex at Lords, Duke Ellington and Ella Fitzgerald at the Hammersmith Odeon; a year later I even queued for four hours to pay homage to the coffin of Winston Churchill, and I was at Wembley to see the start of England's 1966 football World Cup, and Man United's 1968 European Cup triumph.

My father also had a love affair with London, but his focus was the RFU ground at Twickenham. For nigh on 30 years, he would organise the Conservative Club's biennial January trip to London for the Wales–England match.

Once one trip was over, each member of the party would hand my father £5 a week for him to save for the next trip in two years' time. He had great difficulty keeping tabs on all these small random payments, so in later years I had to bail him out on a couple of occasions when the books didn't balance with his bank account. I often wondered why the club members didn't just open a savings account with their own banks. Perhaps this way their wives couldn't get their hands on the money? For all his efforts my father was presented each biennial with an engraved fountain pen by the club members.

The weekend would start at 7 a.m. on the Friday morning when the excursion train left Llanelli station, to return at 8 p.m. the following Monday evening. Wasn't it wonderful having the luxury of a whole extra train laid on just for you for a special event?

My father allowed me, at the tender age of 16, to join the 1960 trip. I remember well the excitement on the Friday morning as not only hundreds of supporters, but countless crates of ale, boarded the excursion train. Who needs a buffet car?

Dad did, however, attempt to protect me from the alcoholic

excesses of the rest of the weekend by dragging me off to the theatre to see *The Mousetrap* on the Saturday evening after the match.

I was later to spend many such evenings in the company of the crowd from Llanelli, when my father still made the biennial trip during my time in London. And, on the Friday evening I would organise a table at the London Welsh gathering at the Seymour Hall. This event, strange to modern ears, was called The London Welsh Smoker. Music, along with alcohol, were however the focus of the evening, with a repertoire which usually included opera singers (on one occasion the world famous Gwyneth Jones) and, of course, the London Welsh Male Voice Choir.

After the weekend's rugby, the Monday mornings of my father's biennial outings were spent shopping, always in Selfridges, buying presents for my mother and aunt, who also lived with us. Such presents were an insurance policy that guaranteed my father's presence on the next trip two years hence.

# 4

# An Exile in London

WHILE MY FIRST few weeks in London were spent taking in the newly-discovered delights of the capital city, I soon infiltrated what there was of Welsh society in the metropolis.

This was partly out of necessity. The few friends I knew were obviously from home, and office workers in such a large city tend to travel long distances into London from all parts of the compass. Hence socialising was a quick pint after work rather than a meeting later in the evening.

I was invited to play cricket at weekends by a friendly fellow worker from Essex, but the initial reaction of some of the office staff to me was one of being introduced to an alien from another planet. One clerical worker – a fat, not too bright girl from the East End – claimed to have never before encountered a Welsh accent, and struggled to believe that there were other similar-sounding human beings to be found somewhere west of London. The Welshness of my accent has partially diminished over the years, although later management associates did observe that it became more pronounced under the pressure of a major presentation. The Welsh preacher in me then tended to emerge.

Another, more erudite, work colleague eschewed Dai as my most obvious nickname for 'Iacky', his bastardised version of the Welsh *iechyd da*.

The office was run by an odd combination of an ex-public school boy for whom work was an irritating intrusion into his cricket and horse racing addictions, and a pompous, overweight, strangely hyperactive, orthodox Jew, who disappeared early every Friday afternoon, suddenly and with no warning, to ensure he arrived home before sunset. Both, I felt. looked down on me.

On first arriving in London, accommodation was not easy to find, and the first few months were spent sharing rooms in a lodging house in Chalk Farm with transient room-mates of every conceivable nationality, including a German (the son of a Luftwaffe pilot), a Dutchman, and a Turk who walked around in two overcoats complaining bitterly about the cold. All three were dragged along to see London Welsh play at Old Deer Park.

The rest of the house, and the several houses alongside, whose residents all ate in our breakfast room, seemed to be mainly of either American or Russian nationality, almost coming to blows at the breakfast table during the 1964 Olympic Games.

During this period, the focus of my week became the Saturday pilgrimage to Old Deer Park. This involved the game, a few pints in the old clubhouse, standing under the 10-foot long red dragon which was suspended from the ceiling, the frenetic perusal of the Saturday pink version of the *Evening Standard* for the Scarlets' result, a trip into King's Cross to the Saturday 'hop' (a term used before disco and rave but postdating prom and dance) at the London Welsh Centre in Gray's Inn Road, and the last tube home from King's Cross with a copy of the first edition of the Sunday papers in tow.

The London Welsh Centre had strong chapel connections so at that time was, unfortunately, not licensed. By the time a bar was opened in the mid 1970s, the interest in the hop had long disappeared, so the demand for alcohol was less. The bar is still active today however, at least on choir practice nights.

I met Graham at the London Welsh. He only stayed in London for 18 months, but during that time he chauffeured one and all from Old Deer Park to Central London each Saturday night. He also drove us home to Wales for many Cardiff rugby weekends. Typically, the route from London to

Wales was tortuous. In the days before the M4, the A4 only went to Bath and Bristol and the A40 stopped at Cheltenham. After this it was cross-country via Hereford to reach the Heads of the Valleys three-lane road. We would religiously stop for a pint at the first pub across the Welsh border, in the little village of Skenfrith. But around Hereford it was all winding country lanes, and Graham drove on the theory that cars would only appear from the other direction on every fourth bend; so for the other three bends overtaking was permissible. He survived, later to be best man at my first wedding.

In those days Llanelli also had at least half a dozen matches a year in the London area, so true Scarlets fans would not be at Old Deer Park on these occasions. The exception was the second Saturday in October when Llanelli were always up playing London Welsh. A marquee was installed to cater for the extra crowd, and the *Sunday Express* announced one year that 10,000 pints had been sold by 6 p.m. Even my parents' annual visit to London was arranged to coincide with this major event.

I was lucky and privileged to follow what were at the time the two best club teams, bar none, in world rugby. Together with Wales, all teams I supported played in red, and one year I never saw any of them lose throughout a whole season.

The attention given to Welsh rugby in those days was greater than today, and Llanelli seemed to appear on *Rugby Special* on Sunday teatime television practically every other week. The Saturday edition of the *Evening Standard* was not however so focused. England is a football-dominated market, and the stop press columns had to be scoured in minute detail to find any mention of rugby results.

Radio was worse, with the BBC Welsh Service almost inaccessible, occupying, as it did, a very similar wavelength to BBC London. On the one occasion I didn't return home to Llanelli to see the Scarlets play a visiting southern hemisphere touring side – in 1970 when the South African Springboks were the opponents – I sat in the car park of the RHM offices in Harlesden, desperately trying to tune into the game. Llanelli had a last-minute conversion to win the game, but it was 15 minutes later before I was able to rejoin the commentary to hear the result. We lost, but times were generally good, with victories over both the Australian Wallabies, three years earlier, and the New Zealand All Blacks in 1972.

If it seems at times that I am addicted to rugby, it is perfectly true. In the 1956 Llanelli Grammar School magazine I was quoted as being the only boy in school who was purported to argue furiously about a rugby match played as long ago as 1905. This, of course, was a reference to New Zealand's disallowed try in Wales's famous victory in a game then dubbed as 'the championship of the world'.

I read once that there are more Welshmen in London than in Cardiff, but unlike the other nationalities – the Irish in Kilburn, West Indians in Notting Hill, the Jews in the East End and now in north London and Hertfordshire, Asians in Southall – the Welsh have not created their own ghetto. Perhaps there are not enough of us? Small exceptions are Paddington, where every hotel is Welsh-run, and Harrow, where we were probably attracted to the hill.

Most Welsh, however, are to be found in similar professions. Every milkman and teacher in London used to be Welsh. And the latter, in particular, provided a substantial reservoir of talent for the great London Welsh rugby sides of the 1960s and 1970s. Welsh teachers sadly can no longer afford London house prices, and this is reflected in London Welsh's long-term rugby decline.

While the Welsh don't live together, they need no excuse to get together, mainly to drink and sing. Each weekend, there were designated pubs where the presence of Welsh people was guaranteed. On Fridays, on a small scale, there was the Bird in Hand in Hornsey in north London. On Saturdays, after the rugby, we would retreat to the Cock Tavern in Great Portland Street, designated the central London headquarters of the London Welsh rugby club. From there it was on to parties in

Kilburn, Hampstead or Hammersmith, or even to the Barts Hospital nurses' disco.

There were also a host of Irish folk pubs in west London if we felt like a change of Celtic scenery. We were all big Clancy Brothers fans at the time.

Friend Graham, as well as providing transport into town, also had a quartet of Pembrokeshire mates who lived in a small terraced cottage off Black Lion Lane in Chiswick. They used to leave their living room window ajar for us to clamber in to find a sofa or bed for the night if the Saturday party happened to be in the centre of town and we were too late to catch the last train home.

One of the cottage's occupants was Merv, a dustman who was ever so proud of being responsible for emptying the bins of John Thaw and Sheila Hancock who lived just around the corner. I have recently learnt that Merv is now an HM Inspector of Schools. Didn't I tell you that Welsh dustmen were bright?

Sunday evenings was the turn of the aptly named Prince of Wales in Drury Lane, off Covent Garden. Here was a different clientele, worshippers from the various London Welsh chapels, who would congregate after evening service to continue their singing under the conductorship of Dai, later to be known, after several illnesses, as 'Dai Heart Attack'. The venue was so popular that it was actually difficult to get in through the door.

At that time, in the late 1960s, I shared a flat with three Welsh guys in Finchley, with two being Welsh speaking. So I was becoming more Welsh than ever.

I then met my first wife, Catherine. This was at the Cock Tavern, although Catherine wasn't Welsh, but first generation Irish from Lancashire. She did however share a house in South Harrow with two Carmarthenshire girls, and we lived in Harrow when first married. So I became introduced to the Harrow Welsh Society, to the chapel, to the St David's Day dinners, and to the John Lyon pub on a Thursday evening.

I never attended the chapel. I did however attend a few Welsh-speaking classes run by the minister, and regularly played table tennis for the chapel team in the London Welsh chapel league. I was amazed to discover there were in excess of a dozen Welsh chapels spread across north and central London, including Haringey, the King's Road, the Barbican, and Baker Street (in a building later to be shared with a Chinese church).

I was a table tennis addict, first introduced to the game in the hotels of Bournemouth on the south coast holidays of my childhood, with my interest nurtured by YMCA, church youth club and university. My father had also played the game at the YMCA, and in my study I still proudly display his runner-up cup from RAF Birdlip in 1942. He claims he would have won if he hadn't just come off night guard duty.

I have played competitive league table tennis for nigh on 50 years, apart from a 15-year gap when I sampled the more energetic delights of squash. Such competition involved a variety of different north and central London leagues, so the London Welsh chapels league may not have represented the highest standard of play, but its annual singles and doubles knockout competitions played in front of upwards of 60 spectators in the hall of Willesden Chapel, then the home of the only Welsh-speaking school in London, was certainly the most compelling event I encountered. I twice reached the final, only to lose on both occasions.

The Welsh chapels also jointly owned a rather large piece of real estate hidden behind a square of large detached houses in Cricklewood. Here was to be found the Cambrian Lawn Tennis Club. I played at the club spasmodically over a two-year period in the early 1970s, and actually managed to win a singles trophy on this occasion. I however fared less well in the more competitive environment of other more established north London tennis clubs, with just two handicap cup wins to my credit, plus captaining Radlett's third team in its descent from division four to division six of the Hertfordshire League.

At Harrow Chapel I met my longstanding friend, Keith

Thomas. Keith was born in Swansea, a fact which I will gloss over, but the family moved to England when he was young as his father pursued a lecturing career, eventually becoming principal of Uxbridge College. As a consequence, despite his parents being fluent Welsh speakers and several attempts at Welsh lessons, Keith has no Welsh language.

Keith however feels Welsh, and has maintained his father's life membership of London Welsh Rugby Club. I have occasionally had doubts about Keith's Welshness as, if truth be known, he prefers football to rugby, being a keen supporter of Man United, and I once recall him actually falling asleep in front of the television during a Wales–Argentina Rugby World Cup game. To be fair to Keith, the game was extremely boring.

Keith's father used to meet up with various Welsh cronies at the John Lyon pub in Harrow every Thursday evening. Among his acquaintances was the well-known conductor Owain Arwel Hughes, now a CBE, who once hosted a Sunday night TV series called *The Best Loved Music Show*, which apparently was a favourite of the Queen Mother.

Keith and I often joined this gathering, together with my father when he was up in London. On one occasion, my father and Owain got into conversation about the relative merits of the various choirs that had competed the previous week for the National Eisteddfod's chief male voice choral award. My father was critical of the judges' decision, and asked what right Owain had to so strongly support the winning choir. Owain quietly announced that he had been the chief adjudicator. I cringed and disappeared to the gents.

Also in Harrow lived 'Dai Boxes', the son of the local undertaker, and 'Arthur Dail' (Arthur Leaves in English), whose name we translated into Welsh because he had taught himself Welsh out of a book after a childhood spent in Cardiff speaking English. As a consequence, my Welsh-speaking father couldn't understand a word he said. *'Pwy yw hwnna?'* (Who is that one?) my father would say to me. Yet Arthur would still persist in speaking Welsh at every opportunity, even to my Anglo-Irish wife, who obviously also couldn't understand him.

Arthur was a permanently suntanned bricklayer with an eye for the ladies, who played squash and table tennis well into his seventies, in earlier years even winning the coveted London Welsh chapels table tennis singles. He also once called round at my house as I was leaving to take two suits to the jumble sale, took a fancy to the two suits and promptly walked off with them. Arthur died in 2009 having achieved a century of years.

As the years of married life passed by, and we moved to Bushey, near Watford, my contact with Harrow Welsh declined. I didn't even see young Keith for almost ten years. Apart from trips home to see my widowed mum, my only Welsh contact was infrequent visits to watch London Welsh play rugby at Old Deer Park in Richmond. Then, I came across the bowls club.

# 5

# The Bowls Club

LONDON WELSH RFC, in these professional times, spares no effort to make visitors and opponents welcome. There are bars in the clubhouse, around the pitch, and in a hospitality marquee where all are free to reserve tables of ten for pre-match meals with guest celebrities and entertainment. There is also a hog roast and a very good food-bar for more casual eating.

But in direct contrast to what I have always regarded as the innate friendliness of the Welsh, the same rugby club, around 1980, at the height of its popularity as London's most successful team, went through a phase of being less than friendly. While other London rugby clubs such as Wasps, Richmond and Saracens welcomed supporters with open arms, even into the more exclusive sections of their clubhouses such as the President's Bar, the London Welsh suddenly adopted a more austere approach to visitors, placing bouncers on every door, allowing only the *crachach* (snobs) into the John Dawes Room, only season ticket holders into the members' bar, with non-members and visitors being forced to drink in a makeshift bar in what was the tea room.

While Keith was a longstanding season ticket holder, I only joined for a solitary season. So, on one occasion, a bouncer prevented me as a non-member from entering the members' bar to share a drink with Keith.

Other supporters, when similarly treated, retreated to the far corner of Old Deer Park, and the Mid Surrey Bowls Club. The club, which also at the time had a Welsh president, enthusiastically grasped this opportunity to boost its funds, and proceeded, on every home match day, to set up two real ale barrels at each end of the bar counter, and furnish the London Welsh supporters with a home from home. Even the club's most famous player, Wynne Richards, a winner of the world renowned Kodak Masters, hailed from Wales.

The bowls club in the early 1980s became the place to be. The second team drank there. London Welsh 'choirboys', i.e. members of the London Welsh Male Voice Choir, congregated there when they had no concert that weekend. Dignitaries such as Neil Kinnock and Owain Arwel Hughes drank there. Visiting supporters, including the famous Mrs Mainwaring of Aberavon, soon appeared there. The place would be full, standing room only, with the walls reverberating to song, helped by the acoustics which were far superior to the low ceiling of the new rugby clubhouse, which had replaced the old wooden structure and its 10-foot suspended dragon in 1969. (Only a Welshman would worry about acoustics.)

The singing was led by Dai Heart Attack of Prince of Wales, Covent Garden, fame. Dai would spend half an hour warming up in the corner, indulging in obscure Welsh *penillion* (stanzas) singing with his north Wales cronies, and then climb onto a table and lead the packed gathering in more well-known hymns, sang, in what he liked to call 'God's own language'.

When members of the London Welsh Male Voice Choir were present, they sometimes liked to do their own thing, and as this involved 10-minute gaps between songs, they often found themselves in competition with a breakaway noise from elsewhere in the room. Dai was the unifying force that pulled everybody back together, although the choir did get a little precious one season, when they retired to sing on their own in an outbuilding which served as the home bowls team's dressing room. This immediately became known as 'the inner sanctum' into which one could only enter by invitation.

Attendances have since flagged as the fortunes of London Welsh dipped with the commencement of national leagues, with the team descending one season to the depths of Division

Five South. They have since recovered to the respectability of National League One, now rebranded the Championship, but are not as yet a match for the professional teams in the Premiership.

Although the bowls club is still reasonably full after home games, most people are now able to find a seat, as opposed to the once standing room only. I have graduated into the 'inner circle' who sit centre table leading the now more sedate, less mass, singing, occasionally attracting a few 'choirboys' over from the main clubhouse to provide depth and substance. We are known, I discovered recently, as 'the deacons', our table being seen as similar to 'the big seat' that deacons occupy in front of the pulpit in a Welsh chapel.

This inner circle of deacons is largely made up of ex-Osterley RFC players from west London. Although in their sixties, they still indulge in rugby training in an Ealing gym every Wednesday evening. They hail originally from Seaside in Llanelli, the Pembrokeshire holiday resort of Tenby, plus a few Newport, Gwent, boys and north Walians.

Even though we only frequent the main clubhouse for a few minutes before every home game, we are still very friendly with the London Welsh supporters' club, who do good work, organising pre-match gatherings in the City Hall before all Welsh games in Cardiff, and producing a useful 'little red book' containing the words of all the hymns and songs that form part of a Welshman's musical repertoire.

Mike Hynes, once secretary of the supporters' club, now sadly deceased, was a sort of honorary deacon, often joining us in song, and, as a Welsh-speaking west Walian, often providing us with the more obscure additional verses of various Welsh hymns which, if truth be known, we were not actually that keen on singing in the first place, given that we didn't know the words.

Another stalwart and hard-working member of both London Welsh choir and supporters' club is Martin 'Joe' Jones. Joe also finds the time to edit the supporters' club regular newsletter, and has recently become the design and publicity manager of the rugby club itself.

Mike and Joe both lived on the Kew Road alongside the London Welsh ground. One could in fact be forgiven for believing that the whole of the supporters' club did as well, as that wonderful pub called the Shaftesbury, just short of the Kew roundabout, which we visit before every home game, always seems full of Welshmen. This, even on a Friday evening in midsummer, when the deacons meet up for a between-season reunion drink.

The Shaftesbury is yet another home from home for Welshmen, and at the pre-match gatherings you can almost hear as much Welsh being spoken as English. The English often maintain that this only occurs when an Englishman enters the pub. How do they know this? They can't be in the pub before they've entered it. And anyway why can't a Welshman speak in his own language? They don't expect the French to speak English in Paris... or, on second thoughts, perhaps they do?

For my part, I have no qualms about allowing Welsh speakers their once-a-fortnight opportunity at the London Welsh to converse in their native tongue, even if I can only understand snippets of the conversation.

If London Welsh were ever to reach the dizzy heights of the Premiership they would in these professional times have to find a bigger (probably football) stadium, to accommodate the larger crowds. This would all but destroy the social scene that has built up around Old Deer Park, the bowls club and the Shaftesbury pub. We aren't certain that we really want this to happen.

To return to the bowls club and the deacons, just as American football teams rely on their quarterback, so does any impromptu choir rely on its pitcher, so that we tenors are not left gasping for air as we strain to reach the last and usually highest notes of the hymn. In the pubs surrounding the Millennium Stadium in Cardiff, the singing, or should I call it screeching, is always unfortunately pitched too high by a valley boy who thinks he's a boy soprano when he actually sings bass.

The first bowls club pitcher was Dai Heart Attack. After his sad demise, he was replaced by Ken Barrington, the then London Welsh official photographer. Ken is survived by his son, Huwie, famously known by supporters throughout the whole of the Championship for his non-stop touchline barracking of officials and opposition, which one day will result in either a coach or a sin-binned player causing him serious bodily harm. A fellow supporter has now supplied us all with a sort of bingo card to see who can be the first to hear, and tick off, all of Huwie's favourite sayings in the one match.

Our new pitcher is Alan Cole of Seaside, Llanelli. Alan is a keen folk singer, even managing to make 'Cwm Rhondda' sound like a folk song. We lost Alan on a recent trip to a Wales–Ireland international in Cardiff, only to find him holding forth in the hotel bar, entertaining a group of Irishmen with a solo of Irish folk songs. They were eventually allowed to join in as well. The evening ended with the Irish and the Welsh taking musical turns, although at the request of the Irish, the Welsh weren't allowed to sing hymns. 'Please, no hymns!'

Alan shares a surname with my mother, and was also born in the next street to her. On first meeting him I was convinced he was a long-lost cousin. But my mother then informed me that she did remember there being other Coles in the neighbourhood, but obviously not of her pedigree and bearing.

Another Alan, Alan Rees, is the group's main tenor upon whom I rely totally as, although possessing a reasonable tenor voice, I am completely incapable of harmonising without someone to follow. This proves difficult, as Alan, despite his 80 years, is continually leaving our group to roam the bowls club in search of the fairer sex to whom he can be heard reciting love poems in Welsh.

Alan is our main academic and Welsh speaker. He has even toured the pubs of Wales collating a dictionary of Welsh colloquialisms for S4C, the Welsh-language TV channel, and once asked a question from the audience on their Welsh equivalent of *Question Time*. He is happy to lend you a DVD of the programme, if you ever wish to see it.

A former academic colleague of Alan's is Jim 'Third Verse' Jenkins from Tenby, so called because of his encyclopaedic knowledge of pop songs, in which he leads the deacons in singing. The pop songs to which I refer, however, were hits from before 1965, sung by the Everly Brothers, the Beach Boys and the like. Jim's post-1965 knowledge unfortunately doesn't even extend to the names of bands or groups, let alone the lyrics of their songs.

Also from Tenby is Mike Howells. Mike is not however always in regular attendance at the bowls club on account of his frequent holidays abroad. This goes someway to explaining his almost permanent suntan, which I initially thought was the result of him coming from Tenby.

Another Seaside Llanelli boy is Wilbur. As an ex-Llanelli Grammar first team player, with experience of coaching I've been told, Wilbur (his real name, seldom used, is Graham) is the font of all rugby tactics and strategies. The touchline always awaits with expectation his judgements on the play. I think the word 'critic' was invented for Wilbur, as he is forever critical of the London Welsh (not to mention the Scarlets's and Wales's) performance. Wilbur's pint is always half empty rather than half full, although he almost seems happy when his team is losing. The tactical solution to the team's dilemma can then be proclaimed by Wilbur, while the players have still to discover it.

The third deacon with Seaside connections, albeit first generation, is Peter Barry. Peter eats for Wales, so usually bypasses the pre-match gathering at the Shaftesbury in favour of sausage and chips in the rugby club tearoom.

The rhythm for our singing is provided by Lyn, a drummer with a rock band, who uses an empty pint glass to beat out a rhythm on the table. This is highly preferable to a choirboy nicknamed 'Newport' providing us with a beat by hitting all available heads with a beer tray borrowed from behind the bar.

Also hailing from Newport, Lyn leads us in an eclectic mix of solos ranging from 'Lilies of the Valley' to the 'Banana Boat Song'.

The deacons are a mix of Welsh and non-Welsh speakers. Alan Rees, from the Amman Valley, and the two Seaside boys, are fluent Welsh speakers. The rest of us have had to phonetically learn the Welsh words of most of the popular Welsh hymns.

While the Welsh Cup was still a worthy competition competed for by all the senior clubs in the Principality, the deacons used to make an annual trip to Cardiff by minibus for the cup final. Our singing was welcomed in the pubs of Cardiff, even to the extent of being offered free sandwiches to return the following year. This is perhaps the value of a pitcher compared to the boy sopranos from the valleys screeching out their songs on international day.

It is always said that the exiles of different nationalities are more nationalistic than those who stay at home. Perhaps it's also true of singing in the case of the Welsh – although our best evenings in Cardiff occurred when we shared a pub with another club: one year the Whitchurch Cricket Club from Cardiff itself, another year the Birmingham Welsh Society. In both instances, we were still singing two hours later.

Sadly, with the reduction of senior teams to just four Welsh rugby regions, the Welsh Cup has been devalued, now only involving the semi-professional sides of the lower level Welsh Premiership. It is no longer a major event, attracting only a 8,000 gate compared to the 60,000 of its heyday.

Professionalism also threatens the existence of London Welsh and the bowls club. The standard of play has been deteriorating since the 1970s, with far fewer Welsh exiles appreciating the expense of living in London. In addition, the demands of competing in the professional era have meant that the club has had to look outside the Principality for its players.

Originally, to play for London Welsh one had to be of Welsh descent or to have played club rugby in Wales, even if the latter rule was manipulated on occasions by sending a good English or overseas prospect to play in Wales for a fortnight.

But with professionalism the club has had to cast the net wider. And the consequence of this is that there are far fewer players who are Welsh or of Welsh descent. And even the former either do not speak Welsh or have no knowledge of Welsh religion and its hymns.

But all is not lost with the club's supporters. Dr Haydn James, until recently leader of the London Welsh Male Voice Choir, was instrumental in helping to create a British Lions Choir, which has accompanied the British Lions rugby team on its tours of Australia, South Africa and New Zealand. This choir, with a large London Welsh contingent, has graced all the major concert halls, cathedrals and rugby grounds of the southern hemisphere.

There were, however, London Welsh choirboys who didn't relish such a dedicated programme of concerts while on a rugby tour, preferring the option of singing more informally in the rugby clubs of the various countries. Hence, for the 2005 British Lions tour of New Zealand, the London Welsh Rugby Club Male Voice Choir was born. One of the main instigators was, yet again, Joe Jones. Is there no limit to his drive and skill?

The choir has continued in existence subsequent to the tour, accommodating not only exiled Welshmen and first generation Welsh, but also several English supporters who follow the London Welsh rugby club. I have thought, on a couple of occasions, of putting myself forward, but then discovered that it is a choir of very high standards which sings separated into quartets, each comprising bass, baritone, second tenor and tenor, rather than allowing the whole choir to divide into its different voice parts. With my inability to sing in harmony without supporting voices, this might prove a little too demanding.

I have thus contented myself with the twice-monthly Welsh fix I get at the bowls club. The only problem is that we are not getting any younger, and the exile base is getting smaller.

The ageing and decline in numbers of male voice singers is however not a phenomenon that is exclusive to the bowls club. It can be found in most of Wales's long-established male voice choirs. But our musical heritage is still in good hands. S4C's *Côr Cymru* choral competition has showcased for me the exciting youth and mixed choirs that have burst on the scene, developed by really talented and motivated conductors, such as Cordydd of Cardiff, conducted by Sioned James, the youth and children's choirs of Ysgol Gerdd Ceredigion, brilliantly led by Islwyn Evans of Newcastle Emlyn, and Cantata girls' choir, created by Catrin Hughes of Ysgol y Strade, Llanelli's Welsh-language secondary school. BBC's *Last Choir Standing* heralded two Welsh finalists in Ysgol Glanaethwy stage school from Bangor and the now internationally known Only Men Aloud, conducted by Tim Rhys Evans who continues to maintain tradition with his latest venture, the 200-strong Only Boys Aloud.

The Welsh have not been slow either in competing prominently in the more mainstream dance and reality talent shows on network television, or in producing a string of iconic rock and pop bands. This is not confined to the English language, with *Maes B* (Field B) creating a sort of Welsh mini-Glastonbury at the National Eisteddfod.

London is also playing its part, with four resident choirs at the London Welsh Centre – three traditional male voice choirs, the London Welsh, London Welsh Rugby and Gwalia, and Chorale, an exciting mixed choir whom you may have heard backing the opening credits on every European Champions League TV transmission. And finally we have Eschoir, a young male voice choir in the manner of Only Men Aloud.

Our musical heritage is hopefully still alive and kicking.

# 6

# Welsh Addictions

I HAVE INHERITED many Welsh characteristics, both good and bad.

The Welsh are firstly a nation of hypochondriacs. They account for more GP surgery hours per person than all of the rest of the UK.

While working at H J Heinz, a female colleague of mine spoke of her Welsh aunt writing to her mother. The first few paragraphs of every letter always read like a hospital bulletin. The English talk about the weather. The Welsh talk about their illnesses.

I am also a hypochondriac, and this is as a result of environment as well as heredity. At the tender age of two-and-a-half, I fractured my femur after a bad fall. On examination, it was discovered that the fracture was caused by the existence of a cyst, with which I had apparently been born. I therefore had the cyst removed from my upper leg, and replaced by a bone graft taken from my lower leg. Not a simple operation in the distant past of 1945.

The operation, plus an extended period of convalescence, meant a hospital stay of the best part of a year. This was followed by 18 months in a calliper, worn throughout the day and night.

Both operation and convalescence occurred in Cardiff, 50 miles from home. Travel was difficult, as it was wartime, my father was away with the RAF, and we didn't own a car. So my mother wrote for information about the operation, and received this handwritten letter from the surgeon a week or two later:

*Dear Mrs Daniels,*

*I must apologise for not answering your letter sooner. I was hoping to have some news of Peter's X-ray before writing, but as you apparently know by now, he was transferred to the country branch at Crossways.*

*You should have been notified about this through the office. In case you have not been informed, you can visit Peter on the last Saturday of each month, unless of course there is some infection there. Should this happen, the parents are informed. The Ward Sister will then tell you personally how Peter is getting on. When you visit him I hope you will find him getting on satisfactorily,*

*Yours sincerely,*

Child welfare would have a field day with this today.

Mam was fairly highly strung in the first place, and claimed that she herself had been both deaf and blind for short periods in her childhood. My accident must therefore have made her paranoid. Even when she was dying, and her mind was failing, she pleaded with me to believe that my fall had not been of her doing.

I therefore spent my childhood years wrapped in cotton wool. I was one of only two boys in the street not to have a bicycle. I also never learnt to swim. There was, in any case, no local swimming pool, and the only way to learn was to dive off the quayside and mix with the dead dogs in the North Dock. Perhaps I was just a coward?

It was amazing I ever managed to play any rugby, but even then, my mother would send me to school with a note asking for me to be excused showering after playing, in case I caught a chest infection. Of these, I did have plenty. Once or twice a year, I would go down with congestion or bronchitis, which my mother would insist on calling mild pneumonia.

The doctors were just as bad. Such a chest infection would require two weeks off school, the first of which was a statutory seven days in bed, with the windows closed (you could never open them in our house anyway), and a permanent electric fire switched on, even at night.

I was then allowed out of bed for a few days before being permitted eventually to sample the outdoor fresh air. It usually took me weeks to recover, not from the infection, but from the treatment.

I did, through all of this, manage to play some rugby. Picked for the school in my first year at the grammar school, I however came down with a cold just before my second game. My mother refused to allow me to play, but my mistake was to go straight home after school without telling the sports master of my unavailability. 'Thomas Gym' never picked me again.

Almost in retaliation I became addicted to sport of all types, particularly bat and ball sports like tennis, table tennis and later squash and golf.

With the exception of the religion that is rugby, the Welsh, in general, are not great sports performers. With a population of only three million, and not that much in the way of facilities, it is quite difficult to make an impression on world sport.

Our school was divided between two widely separated sites, with sports facilities only available to the lower school. The exception was Thursday afternoons when the senior school could make use of the junior school facilities, if they could be bothered.

But we still took our rugby very seriously. The Llanelli Grammar School sevens team won the English Public Schools Sevens tournament on four occasions in the six years in which they competed. On the first occasion, I remember the whole town knew that we had won within minutes of the final whistle, even in the absence of any media communication. After a further hat-trick of wins, however, we withdrew after being accused of being too professional. The team did actually train every day, including an hour's circuit training each lunch break.

In contrast, pupils were not allowed to bring footballs into the school, even just for the playground. The oval ball was god – although the good rugby players usually played soccer for local clubs on Saturday afternoon after playing rugby for the school in the morning.

As a child I also played a lot of cricket. In fact I probably played cricket more than any other sport, not in any serious competitive way, but with half a dozen friends in the park every day throughout the summer holidays. As a consequence, both my tennis forehand and my golf swing unfortunately resemble a cricket batsman's off-drive.

I can tell you that cricket in the park with just a batsman, a bowler, a wicketkeeper and one fielder is an extremely tiring game, especially for the lone fielder. It was, in addition, in the absence of a formal boundary, difficult to agree on exactly how many runs had been scored.

We also played cricket in the street. The wicket would be painted on the side wall of a house, with the bowler's run up disappearing down the back lane opposite. It was the batsman's responsibility to warn of approaching cars.

Touch rugby was also played in a nearby cul-de-sac, with a school cap as a ball. The in-goal area was again the main road.

But cricket was mainly about watching Glamorgan. On bank holidays most other counties had established permanent fixtures with neighbouring rivals. For example, Gloucester always played Somerset. As relative newcomers to the scene, and without such established fixtures, Glamorgan were lucky enough to be awarded Whit and August bank holiday fixtures with that summer's visiting overseas tourists.

Each bank holiday weekend Saturday thus saw my father and me watching Glamorgan, either at St Helen's, Swansea, or the Arms Park in Cardiff.

I remember on one occasion in Cardiff, Wilf Wooller, the cantankerous Glamorgan captain, England cricket selector and ex-Wales centre three-quarter, coming out to bat and, once at the crease, deciding he had the wrong bat. Returning to the pavilion under the old rugby North Stand, much to the derision of the crowd, he came out for a second time, only to be clean bowled first ball.

One apocryphal story I heard about Wilfred Wooller concerned the occasion of his first rugby cap for Wales while still a schoolboy at Rydal School in Colwyn Bay. On the Friday afternoon before the game, he got up from his school desk to leave the classroom before the allotted end of the lesson. The schoolmaster bellowed 'And where do you think YOU are going, Mr Wooller?' 'To play for Wales, Sir,' came the reply.

Many years later, while recruiting research executives for the market research department at H J Heinz, I encountered a young lady called Wooller, who happened to hail from Cardiff. Very derisively I questioned her: 'you're not related to WILFRED Wooller are you?' 'My father,' she replied. Jackie got the job and we became the best of friends.

The only other sports that the Welsh seem to be in any way proficient are darts, snooker and boxing. The Welsh historian, John Davies, puts this down to the inherent 'beeriness' of the population. Llanelli's profusion of snooker halls has in fact produced two world-class snooker champions, Terry Griffiths and Matthew Stevens. Terry used to play occasionally in the Conservative Club, and I was saddened that my father, who knew him well, died only months before Terry won the World Championship at the Crucible at his first attempt after turning professional in 1979.

Up to the 1960s, Wales also produced its fair share of champion boxers. Boxing was obviously unlikely to be my forte, but in the next street lived Glyn Davies, who once laid claim to the Welsh bantamweight title. Not a big lad, but he packed a punch, and still seemed super fit when I passed him in the street a few years ago. On one occasion I had an altercation in a back lane game of rugby with a lad who was a little bigger than me. Neither of us really fancied the fight; it was really more of a sparring session. But my opponent made the mistake of making a side remark to Glyn who was watching the fight. One punch into the solar plexus, and that was the end of that.

I also remember on another occasion a visit to Porthcawl's Coney Beach, climbing through a gap in the fence to catch a glimpse of Ingemar Johansson winning a European heavyweight bout. But that was where my contact with boxing began and ended.

Rugby, boxing and snooker apart, the Welsh, as mentioned earlier, are not great sports performers. But they are still sports addicts, partly of the couch potato variety, but also as keen live spectators.

My father would frequently return home from an evening at the Conservative Club with yet another programme from a sporting event, passed on to him by one of the members. I thus became a programme 'anorak', collecting programmes from every conceivable sport and era.

My interest was encouraged by my father's Uncle Dan. Dan lived in Dolau Fach, one of the many terraced streets in Seaside, along which the steelwork's shunting engines literally ran past the front doors of the houses. Dan had been bedridden for years and, as a small boy, I used to take my programmes to share with him, so he could recount to me the tales behind the rugby matches featured in my collection.

On my retirement, I have found the time to file and catalogue what has now become quite a substantial and valuable collection. It includes programmes from the London Olympic Games of 1948, a Llanelli v New Zealand programme from 1924, the Cassius Clay v Henry Cooper fight, a dozen or more FA Cup finals, an ice hockey programme from Canada, to name but a few – even an in memoriam card for a Welsh rugby victory over England in 1897.

Allied to their obsession with education, the Welsh have also become quiz, particularly sports quiz, addicts. And not for the Welsh a once-a-week pub quiz night, but serious inter-pub quiz leagues.

Graham, back home in Wales after his 18 months in London, participates in such a league. One day last year, he phoned me out of the blue while we were throwing a dinner party, to inform me that I was his phone-a-friend, feeling sure that I would know the answer to an obscure Welsh rugby question. I am not certain that phoning a friend was a legal part of the proceedings but, ever the anorak, I duly provided him with the answer.

Also, Graham's Oxford-educated son, whenever short of beer money, would spend a few minutes on a pub quiz machine to boost his finances. He always won, so I'm not surprised to see that such machines now have a much more limited pub presence.

Wales is however a matriarchal society. John Winterson Richards' *Xenophobe's Guide to the Welsh* observes that it is run by 'a secret and sophisticated elite, the women. The dominant feature of a Welsh childhood is "Mam". "Dad" is a shadowy figure, always "down the club".'

At home the women held the purse strings. The men handed over their pay packets and were provided with weekly 'pocket money'. From the rest of the pay packet my mother would then save for our once yearly 'upmarket' holiday on the south coast of England.

The *Xenophobe's Guide to the Welsh* also points out that 'Mam is so tough about what is allowed in the home'. In my case, my mother's caution about all things physical also extended for some reason to DIY, and Dad and I were not allowed to touch anything remotely connected with the electricity or plumbing. My father, in fact, had been a RAF radio operator during the Second World War, but this didn't appear to manifest itself outwardly in any electrical or electronic knowledge.

If a TV fuse blew, then it was my fault for having recently changed the TV channels. Goodness knows how my mother would have coped with the intricacies of digital TV, DVDs, computers and the internet, and it is to my permanent amazement that I have acquired some of the technical skills associated with the computer generation. This however only extends to experimenting with the software potential. I am still too frightened to play with the actual physical hardware or wiring.

For most DIY tasks, Dad always knew 'a man who could' from among the hundreds of steelworkers with whom he was acquainted. In my teens I had a short love affair with the athletic high hurdles. My father, bless his heart, thus commissioned one of the steelwork's carpenters to construct a wooden hurdle over which I could train in our back garden. It didn't matter that the hurdle was of a heavy wood construction and not the usual light metal tubing, or that our small lawn only facilitated a six-foot run-up. The dimensions of the hurdle were probably not that accurate anyway. But it was the thought that counted. Dad was always broad of spirit.

To do our painting and decorating my mother discovered a four foot six local woman, aptly named Miss Samson. Peggy Samson was the most dynamic painter and decorator I have ever encountered. She actually had to be, in order to complete her work in the allotted time while still stopping for her very regular tea breaks, during which she would acquaint Mam and Auntie Gertie with all the local gossip and the state of the well-to-do houses she had recently decorated.

The Welsh are born gossips. John Winterson Richards suggests that 'Welsh people routinely start talking with perfect strangers, and not just about the weather. You can end up hearing the life story complete with intimate emotional details of someone you met ten minutes earlier.'

This inquisitiveness might go some way to account for my chosen career of market research, and my desire to experience the larger world offered by London. My work has involved travelling to interview people in all parts of the country and in all walks of life, from six-year-old children, to drug addicts, to high-flying businessmen.

People have always fascinated me, as has the machinations of business with its marketing strategy making, brand imagery, and even statistical analysis. However, my humanist tendencies didn't appreciate the political in-fighting or the single-mindedness required in the drive for both company profit and individual power. Thus, after various senior management positions in blue chip manufacturing companies, and directorships of two market research companies, I spent the last 15 years of my working life as a freelance market research consultant operating from home.

The Welsh are also quite artistic, probably more so than suspected by the rest of the UK, on account of much of it being parochial. Cultural coverage, of such events as national, international and *Urdd* (youth) eisteddfodau, Choir of the Year and Cardiff International Singer of the Year, is to be found in far more profusion on Welsh than English TV channels.

The Llangollen International Eisteddfod is of worldwide renown, with competitors from countries as far west as the USA and as far east as China, but it is completely disregarded as an event by British television. I have however become an avid viewer, now that I can access the Welsh channel, S4C, as part of our Sky package.

My mother was tone deaf, but my father had a pleasing baritone voice. My voice is also reasonable, but totally untrained. I had, as mentioned earlier, rejected the church choir, and school music lessons consisted of our short fat music teacher, nicknamed *Bola* (Welsh for belly), repeatedly playing the same three pieces of music on the gramophone. Over time, familiarity actually generated an affection for these pieces, and I bought 12-inch vinyls of all three: 'Pomp and Circumstance March No. 4' by Elgar, 'The Grand March' from *Tannhauser* and 'Prelude to Act 3' from *Lohengrin*, by Wagner.

I did venture in the mid 1970s to join the London Welsh Male Voice Choir. I was immediately pronounced a second tenor which proved a nightmare to my untrained ear, as second tenors are forever destined to sing the most complicated harmonies, much more difficult than the top tenor part, to the baritone's melody. I persevered, once a week, for six months, but found it difficult to practise between rehearsals in the absence of a piano. We were also expected to memorise the words. I was measured for the choir's red blazer, but never made it on stage, thus missing out on the biennial 1,000 voices concert organised by the choir at London's Royal Albert Hall.

Family commitments meant I was never going to keep up with the choir's demanding schedule. Concerts were monthly, and often meant a weekend away in different parts of the country, plus a week's tour every summer to places like Germany, or even Canada and Australia. I was told recently that it costs in the region of £3,500 per year to be an active choir member.

I made a second attempt to join the choir a few years later. By then, the choir had a new conductor, Dr Haydn James, now well known as the man in the red shirt who leads the pre-match singing at the Millennium Stadium. Haydn had been a contemporary of mine at University College of Wales, Aberystwyth. He actually had played for the university table tennis team, for which I was a permanent reserve. I however beat him on one occasion, in the quarter finals of the University Closed Championship.

I turned up for a choir audition prior to Thursday night's practice, assuming it would be a formality. However, I had passed the time between work and the audition in the local pub. Come the audition and I was in a fairly 'relaxed' state of mind. Haydn played three notes on the piano, all of which I failed to hit. He duly refused my application to join, despite the protestations of half the committee, all of whom were friends. I said it was because I had beaten him at table tennis. In truth, I just didn't hit the notes.

I eventually however did get to sing on stage. My daughter, while at the sixth form of North London Collegiate School, sang in the choir and played in the school orchestra. One Christmas they were performing Haydn's *Creation* and needed some male voices for the choir. I was duly press-ganged into service.

The music teacher had to be Welsh, of course, and he spent several weeks of rehearsals telling us how rubbish we were. On the night itself, and possibly as a result of his tauntings, we actually did quite well. The school chaplain was the only second tenor who had sung the piece before, so immediately prior to going on stage, there was an almighty scrum as we all jostled for position to stand next to him. I have always needed a voice to follow.

While my mother was tone deaf she was however a fine artist, both in oils and watercolour, although her skill was more in achieving a realistic feel of sky, trees and water when copying landscapes, than in creating any original compositions. Nevertheless I've often thought of passing off her copy of Constable's *Hay Wain* as an original.

Most of my interests in visual media, however, had a more modern bias. From an early age I was fascinated by the silver screen, and every Thursday, when my mother and aunt held their knitting circle (these days it would be a book club), Dad and I were shunted off to one of the six local cinemas to see this week's epic. Oddly, performances of the then two feature films ran continuously, so when we entered the cinema, usually at about 6.30 p.m., it would be halfway through the main feature.

The net effect of this fascination is that my market research career has involved mainly investigating the public's reactions to advertising, and encompassed six years working directly for advertising agencies. These six years, during the 1970s, coincided with the golden age of British advertising. Prior to this, advertising had been dominated by the hard-sell, slogan-oriented, American style of advertising, which persisted in merely ramming messages down the public's throat. In contrast, the British advertising industry of the trend-setting 1960s and 1970s set out to attract the attention of the viewer or reader, not by shouting at them, but by providing entertainment. And such entertainment was very much home-grown, focusing on the traits and humour of the UK rather than American audiences.

Two advertising gurus, namely Stephen King and Stanley Pollitt, turned market researchers into 'advertising planners', doubling their salaries in the process. The job of the advertising planner, of which I was one, was to undertake research to clearly identify for the creative writers the key elements that gave a brand its appeal, and then to check out not only that audiences liked the resulting advertisements, but that in each case, the humour or impact had its roots in the brand or product and its selling message. Entertaining the audience was fine, but not at the expense of what was being sold. Hence the planners were constantly at war with the creatives who were very possessive of their advertising ideas which the planners were always amending.

The advertisements on which I worked were very much aimed at a British, not a Welsh, audience. Economics demanded that attention had to be concentrated on the highly populated urbanised parts of the UK, so the limited budgets devoted to focus groups always involved splitting projects between sessions in Greater London and either Lancashire or Yorkshire. The schedule not only excluded Wales, but also the south-west, the north-east, Scotland and even the midlands, which were assumed to fall in between the differing cultures of the north and south of England.

But I did learn a lot about the British character, and however much I have argued the case for there being a difference between the Welsh and English personality, I have also to admit that the UK, in its totality, differs substantially from continental Europe.

All my 30 years or more of working in advertising, in both the UK and continental Europe, has highlighted a more subtle British sense of humour, which the continentals don't always understand. The French and Italians, for all their supposed style and flair, recognise only the most basic slapstick style in humour. And the Swiss just laugh at the obvious. Although, having watched the chat show *Jonathan* on Friday night S4C, there might be a case for describing current Welsh TV humour as also bordering on the childish.

The 1990s and the millennium have unfortunately seen a decline in British advertising. It is sad to report that the growing globalisation of brands and their advertising, not to mention TV programmes, has meant that genuine British, let alone Welsh, culture and humour, is in danger of being drowned in a sea of bland mediocrity aimed at the lowest common denominator.

The general tenor of this book isn't in fact meant to be anti-British or even anti-English, but protective of my Welshness. There are many, including the political party UKIP, that feel that Britain shouldn't be ruled by administrators in Brussels. The desire to be Welsh within a larger Britain is really a variant of the same emotion. It is just that in the one instance it is a case of preserving an identity, in the other it is more a case of regenerating an identity that for centuries has been ignored and, until recently, repressed.

My own attempts to preserve my Welsh identity have led me to learn, or to some extent, relearn, the Welsh language.

And whatever my abilities as a creative market researcher, a linguist I am not. According to my wife and kids, I am probably the male equivalent of Mrs Malaprop.

So what hope is there for me and the Welsh language?

7

# *Yma o Hyd*

DAFYDD IWAN, THE Welsh folk singer, and former president of Plaid Cymru, writes in his folk anthem, 'Yma O Hyd' [Still here], about the struggle to preserve the Welsh language.

We haven't done that badly really, as the language is still spoken by 21 per cent of the population, far more than the proportion of Gaelic speakers in Ireland or Scotland, and in Llanelli it used to be as high as 50 per cent, although the figure had declined to 30 per cent (38 per cent in Llanelli rural) by 2001, with subsequent fears of more rapid decline, partly accelerated by considerable immigration from eastern Europe.

In terms of public government and services, Wales is now bilingual, although this official status has only come about through the efforts of a small Welsh-speaking minority, and achieved despite the protests of non-Welsh speakers, in places like the Glamorgan and Gwent valleys, where people believed this emphasis on speaking Welsh was both a social imposition and a hindrance to job prospects.

The diverse views of the two camps are perfectly illustrated in Alun Richard's biography of rugby great Carwyn James. The two men were lifelong friends but in total disagreement when it came to the Welsh language.

Carwyn was born about ten miles from Carmarthen, in Cefneithin in the Gwendraeth Valley, a mining village with small-scale, less exploited, family-owned pits and little of the English immigration to be found further east in the coalfield. 'He was surrounded by people to whom Welsh was their first language and who, for the most part, would have considered it unnatural to speak any other, unless to strangers or employers.'

A further complication was his family roots in Cardiganshire. Carwyn 'was not encouraged to speak a Welsh tongue tainted with the industrialised dialect of Cefneithin, but the purer Welsh of his parents' county'. The overall result was that Carwyn believed strongly in the 'Welsh condition' and like one of the founders of Welsh nationalism, Saunders Lewis, 'was convinced that the life and well-being of the Welsh language was a central political issue and he regarded the fight for its survival as a crucial aspect of the Welsh tradition'.

Alun Richards counters on his own behalf that this was 'a matter that was totally incomprehensible to Welshmen who were not part of that tradition and never would be. It is a difficult thing to explain to an outsider, how a man can feel a stranger in his own country, and the indifference of many Welshmen to their nation springs from the feeling, often justified, of being excluded, especially from those organisations in broadcasting and education where executive positions and a good many others are reserved for those with bilingual qualifications.'

This was at a time, Alun Richards felt, when 'in the general exodus from countryside to town, the ancestors of most of the indigenous Welsh exchanged their culture and language for English which, until the rise of Welsh nationalism, was generally regarded as sensible, being the simplest road to economic survival'.

For Alun Richards, Welsh had become his 'grandparents' language' with a 'special Sundays-only significance', and quoting Gwyn Thomas's words, 'to have the status of a pet, reserved for occasional greetings'.

But times have changed. Over the last 50 years the nationalists have made major progress in obtaining greater recognition and status for the Welsh language. So, in contrast to my childhood, it is now 'cool', particularly in media-driven Cardiff, for the non-Welsh-speaking middle class to send their children to Welsh-speaking primary schools, and then queue up to learn Welsh themselves to keep up with their children.

But it wasn't always like that. Friend Graham and wife Joy are both Welsh speakers, but, like my parents, didn't encourage their children to speak the language. They did, however, put a value on education, with both children educated in public school and university, their son Mark winning a scholarship to Shrewsbury College before obtaining his degree from Oxford. Ironically, and I feel sadly, both Mark and Dawn read languages, but are not fluent in Welsh.

When I was in school in Llanelli, the Welsh speakers from the outlying villages and the monoglot English speakers from the town centre were segmented into separate classes. Hence I was surprised to learn that Wilbur and Alan Cole from the bowls club, despite being raised in the central Llanelli district of Seaside, are Welsh speakers. Alan Cole claims that having Welsh as his first language was a hindrance to his early education.

Alan Rees, also from the bowls club, grew up in the Amman Valley which, in the last census, was still identified as more than 80 per cent Welsh speaking. When he was growing up in the 1940s, even though English was the language of the classroom, Welsh was the language of the playground, and when visiting Glanaman these days, he still naturally converses in Welsh with his friends in the pub. However, today the reverse has occurred, and children, while being taught in the classroom through the medium of Welsh, speak English in the playground. Despite its official acceptance, Welsh is having to fight against the general globalisation and anglicisation of everyday culture.

Hanging on to the language, and passing it on to the next generation, becomes even more difficult among Welsh exiles in England. Wilbur and his family now live in Staines, Middlesex. On first coming to England, they still spoke Welsh at home, and to their children when they were young. But the children's headmistress had a word with Wilbur and his wife about how little their twins were contributing in class, so for the sake of the children, the family began to speak English more frequently at home. Now, even the parents speak to each other in English at home.

Wilbur argues that being a London Welshman is like being in no man's land. When he returns 'home' to Llanelli he is a visitor, an outsider. In London he is also regarded as different, not English.

I have a Jewish friend, locally in Radlett, who is incapable of having a conversation with me when other people are present, without bringing attention to my Welshness. I have grown tired of jokes about sheep, rain, and more recently, rugby.

If we are to be treated differently, then why not demonstrate that we are different. Thus, the first reason for my learning Welsh is actually to be different. Our Welsh language tutor, James, succinctly, but sadly, describes this as a search for 'otherness'. Fellow learner, Gareth, more positively describes it as the freedom to be whatever we want to be. Nationalists would argue more vehemently that to be a Welsh learner is in fact taking a political stand.

Secondly, in Welsh classes, even learners from no longer Welsh-speaking areas like Pontypridd and Porthcawl, speak of a desire for *hiraeth*, a longing to re-experience all things Welsh, to arouse the passion and the pride of being Welsh, so typified by that ultimate Welshman, not long deceased, Ray Gravell. A fellow Welsh learner from Llanelli describes learning the Welsh of his father as filling a gap that he feels exists in his personality.

The third emotion is one of guilt. Two events in my life, one recent, the other from my childhood, highlight this. I have already mentioned that my grandfather owned a team of heavy horses stabled close to our house. After the horses had long gone, the stables were still put to occasional use. When the circus was in town, they were sometimes used to house their animals, including the elephants. And every winter the onion sellers, the 'Johnny Wynwns' from Brittany, would live in the loft for several months. My grandfather would arrange for their onions to be picked up from the local docks, and they became a permanent feature selling their onions at the local market.

Being Breton, and therefore Celtic, they took to the Welsh language more readily than English. So when the father of the family stood at our front door one Christmas with a present of a string of onions, he spoke to me not in English but in Welsh. So there was I, a 10-year-old Welsh boy, being spoken to in Welsh by a Frenchman, and not understanding him.

More recently, I dragged my English wife down to the Millennium National Eisteddfod, held in Llanelli for the first time since 1962. We really appreciated all the big choral competitions. It was the first time that we had sat in a row identified by the letter 'dd'. And we also had need of a translator to help comprehend the comments of the adjudicators.

We hired earpieces to tune into the onsite translation service. This immediately branded us as non-Welsh speakers. The lady sitting next to me turned to her friend, and, pointing at me, whispered *Sais* (Englishman).

This was a huge blow to my morale. Visiting the eisteddfod in an attempt to hang on to my Welshness, I had been branded a foreigner and worse, an Englishman, because of my lack of language.

My first attempt at relearning what little I knew of the language was in the late 1960s in Harrow where the chapel minister held weekly Welsh classes. However, I only lasted a few weeks. Most of the participants were real beginners, first generation London Welsh, who were amazed at my pronunciation skills. But, after all, I had lived in the country for the first 21 years of my life.

Then in the 1990s my second wife, ever sympathetic to my ambitions, bought me a set of Linguaphone tapes. Sadly, they remained unopened for ten years.

Now in semi-retirement, I have finally taken the plunge at weekly classes, initially at London's City Lit Academy off

Holborn Kingsway, and latterly at the London Welsh Centre in Gray's Inn Road, the very venue where I used to dance away Saturday nights in the 1960s.

Many of the learners at Gray's Inn Road are from fairly non-Welsh-speaking Glamorgan and Gwent. They, like me, are in search of their Welshness, although they have had the motivation and sense to go in search of it at an earlier age than yours truly. They work in parliament, the media or computing. Many, like me, also enjoy a drink after class in the bar, where we are joined by members of the London Welsh Male Voice Choir, who conveniently also hold their rehearsals at the centre on Thursday evenings. My wife can't understand why, if the Welsh class is scheduled for 6.30 p.m. to 8 p.m., I do not arrive home until midnight.

The participants at the City Lit classes were also from the educated chattering classes, incorporating trade union lawyers, council administrators and Ministry of Defence librarians in their ranks. Let us hope that the speaking of Welsh is also an aspiration among the true working class, or at least that the compulsory teaching of it in schools will gradually create such a situation.

The City Lit class included several of English descent. Some, like Dave, from Barnet, are keen walkers and campers, holidaying a lot in Wales. Judith, a chorister, plans to move to St Davids in Pembrokeshire. She has an affinity with languages, learning Chinese in parallel with her Welsh lessons. And another girl, a Canadian, was also a 'language tourist', continually seeking new linguistic challenges.

There is always, in each class, one person who more conscientiously insists that we speak in Welsh at all times, including afterwards in the pub. At the City Lit there was Anarchy. I originally thought her name was Anneka, but soon learnt otherwise. A goth dressed all in black with flaming orange hair, she put the rest of us to shame for someone with no Welsh connections, with both her pronunciation and grammar. She eventually left the course because the standard of teaching was not proficient enough for her tastes.

At City Lit our teacher was Glenys, who hails from north Wales with its different accent, vocabulary and grammar. With every new chapter she had to provide us with both north and south Wales versions of the specific points of grammar. You might have thought that only England has a north/south divide. I discovered for the first time that the north Walians' name for us southerners is *hwntws*, which literally translates as 'outsiders'.

Our class textbook was actually entitled *Welsh for North Pembrokeshire and Cardiganshire*. Alan Rees, now of the bowls club but originally of Carmarthenshire, once told me that when sharing digs at University College, Aberystwyth with a fellow Welsh speaker from Pembrokeshire (the next county), the two of them still had great difficulty in understanding each other in Welsh. So much for problems with north Wales Welsh.

South Pembrokeshire is different again, being known as 'little England beyond Wales', mentioned earlier as the source of my mother's ancestry. Alan Rees claims, from his teacher training days following his degree in Aberystwyth, that those sent for teaching practice to Milford Haven, in south Pembrokeshire, were described as being 'sent abroad'.

Richard at the City Lit hails from Pembroke Dock, also in South Pembrokeshire, and he even had problems with the pronunciation, let alone the meaning, of Welsh words. I should worry.

At the London Welsh Centre we are taught by James, who very conscientiously emails us summaries of each week's lesson. Unfortunately my email server fails to recognise the language and deposits all of James missives in the junk mail folder.

Welsh grammar is further complicated by the rules of mutation, in which the first letter of a word is altered when it follows certain other words or phrases. In fact, the same word can be amended in three different ways as a result of three different rules of mutation. Looking up a word in the dictionary when you don't know its original spelling can be something of a nightmare.

And then there are more than a hundred alternative ways of saying 'yes' and 'no', depending on the nature of the question. No wonder we Welsh are ditherers.

But the biggest test for a Welsh learner, again according to Alan Rees, is to be able to converse colloquially in the pub.

Alan has kept his family home in Glanaman, Carmarthenshire, as a second home. He makes frequent visits, so much so, that he has even been accorded the honour of being made president of the local male voice choir.

His local hostelry in Glanaman is the Half Moon pub, and whenever I set out in the bowls club to impress him with my most recently acquired gem of Welsh grammar, he immediately responds by stating that they would never speak like that in the Half Moon, and that I would instantly be identified as a learner of 'book' Welsh, rather than a natural speaker of the language.

Learning Welsh is already fraught with the problems of pronunciation, regional variation, not to mention the rules of mutation. If this isn't enough, my Welsh has also now to pass the Half Moon test.

Nevertheless, *yma o hyd*, I am still trying.

# 8

# God's Country

MY INQUISITIVE NATURE, and the more prosaic need for employment, has seen me spend the last 40-odd years, two thirds of my life, in and around London. But my heart still belongs to Wales.

The Berlin school of psychotherapists in the 19th and early 20th centuries identified what they called the *gestalt* effect, the capability of our human senses to perceive the whole essence of an entity as much greater than the sum of its visible parts. Hence to see a human being is to also immediately be aware of the skin and skeleton encased within its clothes, and the total behavioural pattern of which a human being is capable.

The sight of the Welsh hills generates in me just such a *gestalt* effect. The hills of, say, the Usk valley, or of mid Wales on the road from Llandrindod to Aberystwyth, may be things of beauty, but they are no more attractive than the highlands of Scotland and certainly far less awesome than the mountains of the Canadian Rockies or Nepal. But when I see those Welsh hills I don't just see hills; I sense the presence of banter and laughter, I hear the sound of male voice choirs, and I see every field bedecked with rugby posts. I feel I've come home.

When returning 'home' during my early years in London, I always felt at an advantage to the locals, having sampled a more varied, broader life experience than that offered by the small world that is Llanelli and south Wales. Now I feel envy for those still 'at home', for their more relaxed, friendly existence, in the traffic-free, not unattractive hills and coasts of Carmarthenshire and south Wales.

My mother, on her death at the turn of the millennium, left me a not small, but dilapidated, four-bedroom terraced house in the centre of Llanelli. Given my lack of acquaintance with the skills of DIY, I quickly offloaded the property, for the princely sum of £22,000. And this was as recently as the year 2000.

The family, my wife, children and myself, debated the virtues of using the money as a contribution to a second family home. My inclination was for a two-bedroom apartment on Swansea Marina. The family had a preference for a holiday home in Spain.

After months of excessive debate, house prices had escalated beyond my limited means. My usual ingrained indecisiveness had removed any possibility of a home in Wales. Thus my only Welsh possession, my only remaining piece of Wales, is a pair of debenture seats at the Millennium Stadium.

With my mother's cash we instead purchased shares in the Holiday Property Bond, a wonderful institution which allows us to holiday, at least three times a year, in five-star luxury, in properties throughout the UK, Europe and even the Americas.

Such properties include two Welsh sites, one on a golf course in Beaumaris on the Isle of Anglesey, the other at St Brides Castle in Pembrokeshire.

During a week spent in Beaumaris, I attempted to soak in the Welshness of the golf course views of majestic Snowdonia, and the once-weekly Welsh menu at the onsite bistro of *cawl* (Welsh broth) and Welsh lamb, with even an accompanying harpist.

I also ventured into the local butcher's intent on practising my Welsh, only to learn that the butcher hailed from Somerset. Beaumaris, being quintessentially a holiday town is, in fact, fairly anglicised.

Yet in Menai Bridge, a village not five miles away, we encountered three attractive young 20-year-old girls sat in the local café, conversing fluently in Welsh as their obvious first language. But here I even had a problem recognising that it was actually Welsh they were speaking, given the north Walian accents and grammar. If I hadn't known I was in Wales, they could have been speaking Russian as far as I was concerned.

Are my feelings of Welshness therefore simply an illusion? Not really, as I still managed to feel a sense of pride that my English fellow golfers must have felt that they were in a 'foreign' country, my country. My lack of understanding of the local language was after all something with which I had grown up. The feeling still felt familiar.

The other Holiday Property Bond Welsh property is St Brides Castle in deepest Pembrokeshire. We managed to combine a week in one of its apartments with a few days in Graham's mobile home in the delightful fishing village of Solva, birthplace of Simon Davies (then of Tottenham Hotspur, as the photos and press cuttings on the pub wall constantly reminded us), and also home to the parents of David Gray, the pop/folk singer, who ran the local clothes and gift shop.

Pembrokeshire these days is the ultimate artist's retreat, with countless galleries in St Davids, with the galleries almost as attractive in design as the paintings they exhibit. Not to mention the chapel in Solva, now brightly painted in blue and yellow, and housing the galleries of both dreadlocked Cuban artist, Raul Speek, and his photographer partner. Raul has also combined with a Welsh keyboard player, Roy Jones of Swansea, to produce *Pasaporte para Cuba*, an album of contemporary latin jazz, albeit with a slight Welsh twist.

My namesake, Peter Daniels, was another artist painting in Pembrokeshire until his death in 1998. Descended from a Swansea family, but born and raised in Salford, he moved to Pembrokeshire in 1965 to work as an artist full-time and perfect his vibrant style of landscape painting.

My daughter, Emma, while holidaying at Graham's

mobile home in Solva, was surprised to discover a restaurant displaying an exhibition of paintings all signed by someone called Peter Daniels.

Speaking of restaurants, we have also found Solva and the rest of Pembrokeshire a gastronomic delight. This came as a complete surprise, as despite Wales being the home of some of the world's finest meat and fish, I have never thought of it in terms of its cuisine.

This I partly put down to the available natural ingredients themselves, as with such quality there has never been any need to disguise poor ingredients in exotic sauces in the manner of the French. But it is also partly down to Welsh cooking. All the wonderful fish ends up battered and breadcrumbed in fish and chip shops, and in my childhood, the meat was always overcooked and well done. My earliest experiences were of the cooking of my mother and aunt, so until the age of 20, I assumed that sausages always came with a thick, burnt outer layer of skin. How they were able to cook at all, always amazed me. Our cooker was sited not in the kitchen itself but in an adjoining conservatory (a lean-to really), and the act of cooking was performed under the narrow glare of a household torch.

The new cordon bleu cooking I found in Pembrokeshire is not Welsh-generated but delivered by all different nationalities, with my star going to a wonderful pub in Wolfscastle run jointly at the time by a Frenchman and a Spaniard. And both Solva and St Davids boast several restaurants with stylish modern cuisine. Unfortunately, the prices are modern as well.

Is this another example of my feelings of Welshness being an illusion, or have these immigrants come to Pembrokeshire to perfect their crafts because of the scenery, people and lifestyle that is Wales?

My remaining trips to Wales have focused on rugby, either at the Millennium Stadium or Stradey Park. I grace the Millennium Stadium with my presence on at least four occasions a year, for the Six Nations Championship in the early part of the year, and then for the autumn internationals with the southern hemisphere countries.

On one occasion, for an August bank holiday pre-World Cup friendly against England, my wife and I also extended our stay into a mini holiday, to take in the sights of Cardiff.

Cardiff certainly maintains Wales's reputation as a land of song. My wife and I took in the shops of Queen Street and the St David's Centre on the morning of the match. (I should emphasise that such shopping excursions only occur when my wife is present.) Queen Street was crammed with pavement musicians. There were four separate bands on show, ranging from Irish folk music to heavy rock. And all this while the pubs still echoed to 'Hymns and Arias'.

The morning in addition incorporated an impromptu Welsh lesson as Primark has bilingual signage all through its store. Unfortunately *dillad isaf* doesn't quite cut it as a translation of lingerie.

Cardiff has lots to offer the tourist, and one of my regular daydreams is the possibility of organising holidays to Wales incorporating all the sights, plus golf at St Pierre, Celtic Manor, the Welsh National at the Vale of Glamorgan Hotel, the links at Porthcawl, and the Nicklaus-designed Machynys Peninsula in Llanelli.

Part of the inspiration behind such daydreams is that we Welsh are not that good at selling ourselves, and I want the world to know what a great and friendly place we have in Wales.

I also used to try to make at least one trip per year to Stradey Park, now to Parc y Scarlets, usually to take in a Scarlets European Cup game. We stay at a little pub called Waun Wyllt, deep in the Carmarthenshire countryside, five miles outside Llanelli.

Here you can sit having dinner in the bar on a Saturday night and the only language you will hear spoken is Welsh. In conversation with one of the locals, I referred to an English poem on the wall which joked about Wales being a fine piece of real estate, spoilt only by having horrible (English) neighbours. He looked bemused, and said he couldn't really appreciate it as he couldn't read English.

Not far from the pub is another essential stopping point for my daydream tour of Wales, the National Botanic Garden of Wales. Far superior, in my biased view, to the synthetic Eden Centre in Cornwall. Unfortunately, it is not nearly as well marketed and is continually on the verge of bankruptcy.

But everyone must be encouraged to come to Wales and see it for themselves. Although, I have to admit, that I have heard the occasional story of Welsh people not being that friendly when it comes to welcoming English visitors. Fellow Welsh learner, Jeff, from Swansea, recounts the story of friends from the Thames Valley retiring to north Wales after many happy Welsh holidays, only to move back to Gloucestershire after a hostile reception from Welsh locals. I have even heard stories of a 'two-tier' pricing system, with Welsh shopkeepers increasing their prices on hearing English accents in their shop.

It would be unfair to say that such attitudes are exclusively to be found in north Wales. My wife Gill spoke recently of a conversation with a fellow golfer who had hated her time spent as a student in Cardiff, where she was labelled *Saesnes* (Englishwoman) and ignored by pub barmen as a consequence.

Centuries of English dismissiveness seem to have left some scars. But all visitors must be made welcome, as unfortunately, tourism is the only growth industry in Wales at the moment. Away from the thriving redevelopment of Cardiff, Swansea and Newport, unemployment is high. There are apparently more house husbands than housewives in the old industrial areas of south Wales.

And unemployment and lack of opportunity are no fun. I write this in the week that the 17th suicide of a youngster in a year has occurred in the district around Bridgend in the

Vale of Glamorgan. Not a town with a big industrial past, but a town that has lost a lot of recent industry from such manufacturers as Ford and Sony.

And a receptionist at the Bryn Meadows Golf and Country Club, who has a sister in the police force in Llanelli, recently confided in me that Llanelli is no longer that safe a place for a Saturday night out.

The final, and most depressing, story to emanate from Wales was told to me by English pony trekkers who spoke of locals going 'trekky bashing' in the Brecon Beacons.

Is my Wales only viewed through rose-tinted spectacles?

# 9

# Family Comes First

AFTER THE EXPERIENCE of living with my mother for the first 20 years of my life, I was highly unlikely to marry a Welsh girl.

Dogmatic and obsessive, my mam was quite a handful. I remember one Christmas, when the family (my father, first wife and children) were gathered watching television while my mother was working away in the kitchen, she walked into the living room, studied what we were watching on television, decided she didn't like it, changed the channel, and went back to work in the kitchen.

I wouldn't say she kept the house spotless, but she was obsessive about certain routines, such as systematically vacuuming the dining room floor under my feet every single morning after breakfast.

I have always put down such actions to my mother's idiosyncratic character. But the *Xenophobe's Guide to the Welsh* suggests that she was just being a typical 'Welsh Mam'. The Welsh, it claims, 'do not have the inner compulsion for cleanliness, and the constant discipline required to implement it, that distinguishes nations like the Swiss. But they do have Mam, always a powerful force for order and propriety, who makes sure that when they do wash, they wash hard.'

Propriety was also paramount, and my mother was paranoid, even with our thick net curtains, about neighbours seeing into the parlour window, as it directly overlooked the pavement outside. Switching on the parlour light without first closing the curtains was a crime punishable only by death.

We shared the house with Auntie Gertie, and she and my

mother were again fixated about being fair when it came to sharing costs, even to the extent of having individual saccharin boxes marked with their different initials.

In the kitchen, they also wore overalls to protect their dresses. One Christmas they decided to treat each other to new kitchen overalls, although when preparing Christmas dinner, they both still wore their old overalls over their new, to protect their newly-acquired Christmas presents.

My mother lacked nothing in drive, and despite apparently being a sickly child, she outlasted all her family, living to the grand old age of 90. You could see that she was determined to reach this milestone despite latterly being in some pain. But the year 2000 meant nothing to her, so she didn't hang around for the millennium.

She was obstinate to the last. She went missing from an old people's hospital ward. I spent ten minutes searching the neighbouring streets, thinking she might even have negotiated the locked outer door. She was actually in hiding, behind one of the bathroom doors; she merely wanted to teach one of the nurses a lesson after an argument.

My father could also be dogmatic, at least when it came to arguing about politics or rugby, but he was all talk, as they say, and underneath was an amiable, easy-going man.

The dichotomy of their personalities has probably made me a touch schizophrenic, oscillating between strong-willed determination and total lethargy.

The *Xenophobe's Guide to the Welsh* again suggests that this is not just an idiosyncrasy on my part, but merely being typically Welsh. 'It isn't that the Welsh are lazy. On the contrary, properly motivated, their energy is astonishing, as has been proved on a thousand rugby pitches, in ten thousand pubs, and even in the odd place of work from time to time. The key words are "properly motivated"... If a thing is worth doing, it is worth doing excessively.'

But this dual personality is nothing, according to my daughter, to the contrast in personality between myself and her mother, my first wife. Emma, my daughter, finds it impossible to comprehend how we ever contemplated marriage together.

Catherine is first generation Irish, although with quite a recessive and quiet personality for one of Irish descent. Yet she didn't respond kindly to my occasional rants about the prejudices of the English-dominated press, and on one occasion while holidaying in Cornwall, removed the Welsh flag from among a miniature set of flags bought as sandcastle decorations, and ceremoniously set fire to it.

My second wife, Gill, has been far more sympathetic, encouraging me to learn the Welsh language. She is even attempting to learn the Welsh anthem, 'Hen Wlad fy Nhadau', for her next visit to the Millennium Stadium, although she hasn't yet got past the first line.

She hails from Essex, but after a thorough study of her genealogy, she discovered that her great-grandmother, one Mary Jane Evans, was born in Newport. With such an oft-used Welsh name, she has been unable to trace her lineage back any further.

Gill could in fact pass for Welsh, with her dark hair, brown eyes, melodic alto voice, and creative painting talents.

On the other hand, my own Welsh inquisitiveness has found my first introduction to Essex culture quite an eye-opener.

The Welsh, with their love of education, tend to look down on those who haven't progressed to the higher echelons of the academic firmament. Alun Richards in his short story 'Dream Girl' writes of Dorothea Lemon's carping mother insisting that she wore a uniform despite failing the 11-plus, and warning her off Will Willis, otherwise known as Will Pipes: 'You be careful who you speak to, and come home straight, mind. Will Willis will never get anywhere. He's too half-soaked. He's got plumber written all over him.' Will actually did quite well, running his own business, and employing men, seldom laying a hand on the tools of the trade himself.

Essex is similarly the home of the self-made man, a strong Tory county, the direct opposite of Welshness. When dining with our Essex friends, I discovered that practically everyone's father had run his own business, even if not always successfully. And my two stepsons both left school early, with one now owning a very successful double glazing factory, the other owning a share of a golf franchise within which he is the teaching professional. My kids were, in contrast, university educated, both now working for large companies, one as a finance director, the other as an IT software engineer.

This Essex definition of conservatism is one I have learnt to respect: the freedom and drive to do one's own thing. It is unfortunate that if taken too far, such ambition translates into money at all costs, irrespective of the well-being of your fellow men. And such Thatcherite sentiments have contributed greatly to the current obsession with commercialism and celebrity; not that subsequent New Labour governments did anything to stem this tide.

Essex people in addition love to party. Even on Monday evenings, restaurants are usually booked up. But I think we Welsh are comfortable with this.

My wife and I have actually settled in Hertfordshire, as, when we first met, I needed quick access to the M1 for business travel.

Radlett, Hertfordshire, is a completely different world again. It is 25 per cent Jewish, and as there are two synagogues in the main street, on Saturday mornings it feels like 50 per cent.

Many of our friends are Jewish, and I like their self-deprecating humour, especially the men. While in advertising I worked with many Jewish directors. The urbane Jewish creative writers were a delight with their dry, laid-back wit. But the Jewish corporate bosses, on the other hand, exhibited a far more ruthless streak.

In many ways they are the complete antithesis of Welshness, even more so than Essex folk. They positively encourage chutzpah in their children, which I understand translates as 'aggressive boldness'. And the mothers in their 4x4s must surely have invented the concept of double parking.

The more indigenous locals of Hertfordshire have been brought up in awe of the local TV and film studios in nearby Elstree. (They are actually in Borehamwood, but that doesn't sound as posh.) Neighbour Steve used to work for free on the filmsets during his holidays. And Jewish optician friend, the suitably named Richard Glass, does contact lens work for many well-known Hollywood film stars. So at parties the two sit in a corner debating as to who can claim to have met the most famous celebrities.

Life in general is good, with friendly neighbours, a few very acceptable pubs and restaurants, easily accessible golf and tennis clubs and a small active local entertainment centre. There is even a rugby club, Tabard, which until recently competed as high as National League Three. And memories of my earlier years are evoked by the banter of regulars (many of them Irish) at my local pub.

But I am over an hour's train journey from the bowls club, and, despite England's recent rugby successes, no one in the village seems the slightest bit interested in the game, apart from two Welshmen, plus Danny, an ex-Harlequins hooker who drinks in my local and Rodney, a Haberdashers old boy, who thinks that 'rugger hasn't been the same since the comprehensives started playing it'.

Having now retired, we have theoretically more freedom about where to live, but Hertfordshire is halfway between Essex, and Gill's family, and my two children, both now married and living in the Thames Valley. Moving for the present is out of the question, with Gill's 99-year-old mother and eight (!) grandchildren, and my four grandchildren.

So, living in England, how Welsh are my children likely to be? And what about my grandchildren, the future generation?

An acquaintance in the local pub recently divulged to me that his mother was actually Welsh. This however didn't seem to encourage him to identify himself as Welsh as well. And then I discover he was also born in Abergavenny. 'But that's Monmouthshire,' he exclaimed. So what hope for my brood?

My influence on my children was to some degree limited by my wife and I separating while they were just nine and eleven. They continued to stay with me most weekends, and I hope I have maintained a close relationship with them. But in their teenage years they had to be allowed to build their own lives and develop a relationship with the environment into which they were born and brought up, even if it meant forfeiting their time with me. We Welsh, I hope, are not inclined to encourage a narrow, ghetto culture, to the exclusion of the outside world.

My children were however exposed to the delights of Old Deer Park and the bowls club in their formative years. Initially, Old Deer Park's drawing power was dependent on the quality of the conkers falling from the autumnal trees. Subsequently however, my son did become an avid follower and fan of rugby, London Welsh, the Scarlets and Wales. My daughter rapidly disappeared in the opposite direction. Did I possibly only promote watching rugby as a masculine preoccupation?

My Welshness also surfaced when it came to my children's education, and as someone with socialistic leanings, I had insisted both children went to a local state school. However, Bushey Meads was a bad choice (even if George Michael did go there), and after the school failed to adequately nurture the academic leanings of my offspring, my head ruled my heart, and I paid for their sixth form attendance at Haberdashers and North London Collegiate schools, and subsequent university education.

Gareth, like his father before him, attempted the Oxford entrance examination, but, unlike his father, successfully qualified for the venerable institution, with the help of the highly focused Haberdashers' Aske's school system (25 per cent of the first year intake make it to Oxbridge).

This achievement rightly filled me with parental pride, but it also illustrates how English institutions still dominated my educational thinking. I had bought into the widely-assumed belief of Oxbridge's pre-eminence in the educational firmament. Even in the early days of education in Wales, aspirations (particularly amongst the Anglican clergy) were directed towards the colleges of Oxford and Cambridge, and Welsh university students were originally examined by English university boards.

The preservation of Welshness across the generations requires the maintenance of strong links with Wales or having a local support group for whom Wales and its language are important. Failing these, the single remaining unifying force can only be sport and support for the Welsh rugby team.

I have little or no support group. There remains just the one cousin, with whom I have only recently re-established contact after 30 years of feuding between our respective mothers. (His mother was another version of my mother.) And Jeffrey lives in Kent not in Wales.

On the other hand, my ex-wife, the mother of my children, is first generation Irish, one of six sisters and brothers. By now, there are a multitude of cousins.

Also marrying into a Roman Catholic family meant that the Pope demanded that my children were baptised Roman Catholic. However neither offspring has shown any religious leanings, and both were married, and my first two grandchildren christened, in Anglican churches, purely for convenience.

Both my children have married English partners, one from Carlisle, and one from Yorkshire, the latter even with UKIP members as parents.

Mark from Carlisle is also a sports addict, particularly football. So even though son Gareth and I bought Scarlets' romper suits for Emma's two children when they were born, these days they always seem to be turned out in English or Carlisle football kit.

Emma, in rebellion against having Welsh rugby forced down her throat from an early age, is English first, Irish second, and Welsh not at all. I had to buy her an English replica jersey to celebrate the first of England's Grand Slams in the 1990s. And when I took her to Cardiff for a Wales–Ireland game, she insisted on wearing an Irish jersey, although this only served to encourage every single Welsh fan to chat her up.

Her only Welsh is *'Mae Dad yn talu'* – 'Dad's paying'!

Then, out of the blue, sitting in the car one day, she is word-perfect, singing in Welsh, the first verse of my favourite Welsh folk song, 'Ar Lan y Môr'. Her musical ability is obviously from her Welsh heritage. Her recall of the song, however, only serves to demonstrate how much I must have bored her rigid with it every bedtime.

In contrast, Gareth's best man at his wedding described him as the only Welshman to be born in north London. A Scarlet and Wales fan from an early age, he used to bring all his mates along, many of them Kiwis, to experience the atmosphere of the bowls club.

On one occasion, this coincided with the visit of JPR Williams to his old London Welsh haunts, which also took in the bowls club, such is its popularity. On entering the club, his first visit was to the loo into which Gareth's Kiwi mate, Mark, had just disappeared. Mark reappeared two minutes later, completely in shock at having just had a pee standing alongside the great JPR Williams.

Mark's father had been an enormous fan of JPR and the 1971 British Lions, so despite the fact that it was four o'clock in the morning in Canterbury, Mark immediately phoned his father with the news. The ultimate irony was that his father was really pleased to receive the call, even at that time of night. JPR shook all our hands and signed an autograph for Mark. We really should, however, have put him on the phone to speak to Mark's dad.

When Mark left to return to New Zealand, I presented him with a black sweater bearing the logo: 'Llanelli 9, New Zealand 3 – I was there!' commemorating the Scarlets' 1972 victory over the All Blacks. I really felt it was about time I got rid of it. In return Mark gave me a signed copy of the autobiography of famed New Zealand rugby player and cricketer, Jeff Wilson.

Gareth and his friends really enjoy the atmosphere and

singing at the bowls club. The only doubt I have about Gareth's Welshness is his lack of a singing voice. Mind you, this also applies to Graham and many of my other Welsh friends.

Gareth is still very happy to sit and listen. His interest and belief did, however, waver a little when he became aware of the English translation of the Llanelli song 'Sosban Fach'. What on earth is a war chant doing talking about saucepans boiling over and the cat scratching the baby? Credibility was stretched for Gareth.

But Gareth is a Scarlets' fan through and through, and we have both suffered for the cause, watching the team go down in three consecutive European Cup semi-finals.

The last was at Leicester, to which we travelled with cousin Jeffrey and his two sons. At the game I bumped into the son of my godfather, my father's best man, whom I hadn't seen for all of 20 years. He was also with his two sons.

The five offspring turned out to be all avid Scarlets' fans, attired for the day in the latest Scarlets' replica jerseys.

So there is hope yet?

*Yma o Hyd.*

# Cymro Cymraeg

## Alan Rees

Alan Rees, my rock, my essential tenor support at the Mid Surrey Bowls Club, is an 80-year-old *Cymro Cymraeg*, a Welsh-speaking Welshman, originally from Glanaman, 15 miles north-east of Llanelli in the Amman Valley.

According to the Welsh Academy's *Encyclopaedia of Wales*, Ammanford (*Rhydaman*), at the confluence of the Amman tributary and the Loughor river, was, in its coal mining and tinplating heyday, a major centre of working class Welsh-language culture, and a veritable hotbed of both nonconformist religion and socialism.

With such a strong Welsh language, chapel and socialist background, how do Alan's memories and perceptions of Welshness differ from my more prosaic childhood?

Radicalism, be it of the religious or social variety, is very much part of the industrial Welsh psyche, but, according to travel writer Jan Morris, such radical instinct 'runs deeper than nationalism or economics, and is concerned in all its manifestations with the human condition itself... the Welsh have seldom suffered from national ambition, only national grievances'. Alan's family were at the heart of this radicalism; it partly defined them as Welsh, but it did not focus their minds on their Welshness; they perceived the broader issues of socialism and religion as much more key to their existence.

Alan's family were also fluent Welsh speakers, but the focus here was conversely more narrow. Welsh was the language of everyday culture, not of government or business, and, despite a typical zeal for education, Alan's family did not see Welsh as relevant to either academic study or for getting on in the world. The result has been a widening gap between the colloquial Welsh spoken by Alan and more formal 'book' Welsh. Today Welsh has more status and therefore significance, although at the same time there is still a need for learner classes to focus on the colloquial nature of the more generally spoken language of the street.

Finally, Alan, like myself, has inherited a Welshman's love of rugby, and in this he was also, like me, a Turk rather than a Jack.

Stradey Park, Llanelli 1957

© Tempest Collection, National Museum Wales

Old Castle Works, Llanelli, 1958

© Crown copyright RCAHMW: Dylan Roberts

The North Dock, Llanelli's swimming pool
© Crown copyright: RCAHMW: Dylan Roberts

Dai Losin's football team: Coronation Day Street Parade 1953

Old Deer Park, with the clubhouse to the left and the bowls club directly behind the far posts

Huwie Barrington

Dai 'Heart Attack' leading Ken Barrington and Gomer in the bowls club singing

The author, Alan Rees,
Alan Cole and 'Third Verse'
Jenkins in full voice

The 'deacons' in Cardiff for
the cup: Ken Barrington
(front row), the author, son
Gareth, Jim Jenkins, Alan
Rees (middle) and Keith (rear)

Supporting Scarlets at
London Irish with son
Gareth, cousin Jeffrey and
his son Tom
(with thanks to Ian Williams and
Stradegirl)

Mam and Dad in Bournemouth

With daughter Emma on my 50th

With wife Gill, son
Gareth and his wife
Livvy on my 60th

Five budding
England supporters:
three of my four
grandchildren and
Gill's two youngest
grandchildren

Alan Rees's birthday surprise

The President singing with his choir, Côr Meibion Dyffryn Aman

Level 3 Welsh learners performing a *cydadrodd* (group recitation) with the author (first in line), Richard Williams (third), Dafydd Davies (fourth) and Dai Daniel (fifth)

*Cylch Siarad* (Welsh speakers circle) at the London Welsh Centre bar. Dai Daniel is the fifth face from the right

Tony Fielden supporting Radlett
Cricket Club

Nerys Fielden with Radlett's cricketing wives

Tom Fielden playing for Wales,
cheered on by his sister

Clare Parry

Heinke Pulhorn on the Gower

# 1

# A Turk not a Jack

THE RIVER AMMAN is a tributary of the River Loughor which forms the border between Carmarthenshire and Llanelli on one side and Glamorgan and the new County Borough of Swansea on the other.

I have always joked that the Indian scouts never ventured beyond the Loughor Bridge, leaving the wagon trains to continue unprotected on their onward journey into Llanelli and the 'Wild West'.

But Ammanford and Glanaman are on the cusp. They are east of the Loughor, but the county boundary turns right below the Amman, leaving them just inside Carmarthenshire. The rugby fraternities of Llanelli (Turks) and Swansea (Jacks) have long fought for the loyalty of the valley's supporters. Even today, the newly-created Scarlets region offers the inducement of free coach travel to entice Amman Valley followers to their new stadium, while the rest of us have to pay for the privilege of a park-and-ride.

Alan has however categorically declared that since his youth he has been a Turk rather than a Jack, and even saw Llanelli as a sort of Mecca in his early years. Could this be the same town that my father informed me was affectionately referred to as 'Slash' in the 1940s by the servicemen stationed at RAF Pembrey just down the coast?

As an eight-year-old Alan used to love accompanying his grandmother on her trips to Llanelli market – 35 minutes on the train on what is now the Heart of Wales line running down from Shrewsbury, followed by the trolley bus that met the train and took them up Station Road to the town centre.

Summer holidays from college were spent playing table tennis and snooker at Llanelli YMCA, a place also frequented by both my father and myself. According to Alan's Llanelli mate, so much more preferable to Glanaman Miners' Institute, still 'reeking of the Depression'.

In his teens Alan travelled as far as Llanelli, despite the ribald comments of his friends, just for a haircut. Not the basin cut of Glanaman village barber, Goronwy, for Alan. Ever the elegant gentleman, even today, Alan's hair is always immaculate for his visits to the bowls club.

And such fashion consciousness obviously emanates from his father, who although a radical left-wing trade union official, would often be seen in plus-fours, spats and carrying a silver cane.

Alan's Llanelli haircuts were precursors to glamorous Saturday nights at the Ritz Ballroom. This was the ballroom dancing era, and Alan, later to become chairman of the Aberystwyth College Dance Committee, obviously knew a step or two.

The strategy at the Ritz was to ensure that you at least danced the continental tango with the girl you fancied, as this was the only dance that legitimately allowed you to place your leg between hers.

The big drawback was that the last waltz was at half past ten, only 15 minutes before the last train to Glanaman. But once you started courting, the non-corridor trains back to Ammanford gave plenty of scope for snogging the current girlfriend in its sealed-off compartments. The ultimate part of this strategy was to climb on to the seat and remove the light bulb. I wonder if Alan's grandma would have approved?

## 2

# A Reverence for Education

IN SPITE OF all this socialising, Alan found time to study for a place at the University of Wales, Aberystwyth, following in the footsteps of one of his uncles and two of his aunts.

A university education was always the prime goal for Welsh people; or teachers' training college if you didn't obtain the required grades.

According to John Davies's *A History of Wales*, as far back as the 18th century, Wales was one of the few countries with a literate majority, a *gwerin diwylliedig* (cultured peasantry), partly as the result of Griffith Jones's Circulating Schools, temporary schools which concentrated entirely upon teaching children and adults to read their mother tongue.

The success of these circulating schools, perpetuated by the chapel Sunday school, did much to widen the gap between the experience of Welsh and that of other unofficially recognised languages, such as the other Celtic tongues.

However, in these industrial times, the Welsh also viewed education rather than money as a means of escape from the drudgery and poverty of the steelworks and mines. But in the days before state schools and scholarships, money was still a prerequisite in this search for education.

Alan's grandfather had been a tinplate worker. He also organised a little choral octet which went round the local villages in a horse and buggy giving concerts. On one occasion they were soaked to the skin, a condition which his body found in stark contrast to the heat of the tinworks. He contracted pneumonia and died, leaving Alan's grandmother with four children and one on the way.

Ever resourceful, she opened a shop, *siop werthu popeth* (shop that sold everything). This was quite a common practice among the widows of the area, and there were usually three or four such widows sharing the train on his grandmother's visits to Llanelli market.

With two collieries and a tinworks in the village, the shop thrived, and three of her five children were able to go to college. Specifically to University College, Aberystwyth, as everyone in the Llanelli area went to 'Aber'.

The eldest, Ivor, became a student during the First World War; he was called up, and injured, before returning home to finish his degree. He ended up as head of French in the local grammar school.

But to fund this education someone had to bring in some income to supplement the shop. There were scholarships to be had to Llandeilo Grammar School (no grammar school in the Amman Valley of those days). But this did not pay for uniforms, books or the long train journey to Llandeilo and back. (Ivor would leave home at 8 a.m. not returning home from school until six each evening.)

So the next-born, Idris, had to go down the pit to earn some money. Despite being very bright, and a heavy reader, he had to stay at home with his mother. He never married.

The third-born, Olwen, also went to Aber, requiring the fourth-born, Alan's mother, to leave school early to help his grandmother in the shop. It was the 'luck of the draw', as Alan puts it, dependent on where your birth came in the order of the family.

Olwen became a teacher, but on marrying Herbie, who taught history at Pembroke Dock Grammar School, she was forced to abandon her teaching post, as archaically in those days, married women weren't allowed to teach. Olwen forever resented this situation, being the most intellectual of the siblings, even competing for poetry prizes at the National Eisteddfod. She was also a very gifted musician, accompanying the silent movies at the local cinema when she was just 14 years old.

The fifth and last born was Margaret, Aunty Mag, was also university educated, going on to teach French at Ammanford's Secondary Modern School.

Alan, his grandmother, his mother and father, plus Uncle Idris and Aunty Mag all lived in the same house, built by Alan's great-grandfather on the Square in Glanaman.

With space at a premium, Alan spent the first ten or so years of his life sharing his parents' bedroom. His father died in 1940, and then in 1941, Auntie Liz, who had been made homeless by the Swansea Blitz, also came to stay. So again Alan had to share a bedroom, right up to his 18th birthday, suffering the embarrassment each night of listening to Auntie Liz as she knelt to say her prayers out loud before retiring to bed.

# 3

# Welsh Radicalism

THE WELSH HAVE strong liberal tendencies, a belief in equal opportunity for all fellow men. This has however manifested itself in several different forms, from socialism's efforts on behalf of the working man, to the stand of nonconformity against the excesses of the landowning Anglican church, to the fight to preserve the Welsh language.

These various guises of radicalism must have also come into conflict. For example, the massive Methodist Revival of the early 20th century attempted to ban rugby and close all the pubs. I can't for a second imagine any of the hardened steelworkers approving of this.

Again, socialists like Alan, and his father before him, even as Welsh speakers, had no time for Plaid Cymru (the Welsh Nationalist Party). As socialists they saw the Welsh nationalists as part of the Welsh establishment representing preachers, teachers and literary figures like Saunders Lewis, who were more concerned with the narrow concept of nationalism as opposed to the broader international motivations of socialism.

In later years, by the 1990s, the political environment had changed with the Labour Party moving more to the centre, even to the right, and Plaid Cymru becoming much more left wing.

Ammanford and the Amman Valley were hotbeds of all three radical developments. According to the *Encyclopaedia of Wales*, there was Ysgol y Gwynfryn, which belonged to the tradition of Welsh nonconformist academies in which ministers and eisteddfod performers were trained, while left wing 'workers' forums' were held in a former vicarage called The White House, with Llanelli MP, James Griffiths, among its leading figures. And, as mentioned earlier, Ammanford was also a major centre of working class Welsh-language culture.

The Rees family represented a microcosm of all these developments, and perhaps their conflicts.

Both Alan's mother and Aunty Mag were Sunday school teachers, and there was quite a lot of discussion at home about the Biblical texts they were using to prepare their 'lessons', often consulting a massive book called *Yr Esboniad* [The explanation].

Alan went to chapel and Sunday school every Sunday, and the chapel influence underpinned his attitudes and much of his fluency in the Welsh language. Bible verses had to be memorised by the children who mounted the pulpit at the Bethesda *Cwrdd Cwarter* (Quarterly Meeting). The challenge for the children was to find the shortest verses to limit their stay of execution.

The currency of Welsh culture also flowed through the household. Welsh-language programmes were listened to on the radio; Welsh books were avidly read; eisteddfod results were followed with interest; and there were subscriptions to two weekly Welsh-language newspapers. In parallel, the household (unlike mine) had no time for the royal family, and the King's Christmas broadcast was of little consequence. Later, when Alan joined the British Film Institute in London, he refused to stand for 'God Save the Queen' when traditionally it was played at the end of each performance.

Both Alan's father and Uncle Idris were radical socialists, members of the Independent Labour Party, so the household also subscribed to *The Daily Worker*. Sunday school teacher Auntie Mag was even a member of the Communist Party, adorning the living room wall with a sketch of 'Uncle Joe' Stalin. Alan remembers her having a heated argument with the newsagent when he delivered news of the Molotov- Ribbentrop

Pact, the treaty of non-aggression between Hitler and the USSR in 1939. The household refused to take any newspapers for weeks.

Uncle Ivor, on the other hand, had married Beatrice (Aunty B), a well-to-do shop owner, and had developed somewhat more right wing sympathies after his marriage. They were members of the very active Wesleyan English-language chapel, their religious convictions thus matching their political views. Such politics, typical of the farming gentry of nearby Llandeilo, Alan always felt stood out in stark contrast to the socialist hotbed of Ammanford, even though the towns were a mere seven miles apart.

The household on the Square baked all its own bread, with four loaves also being given to Auntie B. Alan's father likened her weekly visit to pick up her bread as akin to the feudal lord calling to collect his dues from his peasant subjects.

Auntie B and Ivor did their best to prevent the courtship of Alan's father and mother from developing, as Alan's father (plus Uncle Idris) was an atheist, and also a conscientious objector during the First World War. The latter stand was made on political rather than religious grounds, Alan's dad seeing the war as an 'imperialist conflict'. He was not a pacifist however, being a strong supporter of the fight against fascism in Spain, and the war against Nazi Germany in 1939.

Nevertheless he was imprisoned in Dartmoor for 18 months as a result of his beliefs. On leaving the court after sentencing he was pelted with tomatoes, by the deacons of the chapel among others, an event which must have contributed much to his atheist beliefs. Later, he would mercilessly bait the Bethesda preacher whenever the minister called at the house on his pastoral duties.

He was not alone however in his distaste for the conflict in 1914. Even a student magazine in Aberystwyth, *Y Wawr* [Dawn], was closed down by college authorities in 1917, because of its criticism of the war.

According to John Davies, in *A History of Wales*, it was

reasonable to assume there would be many in Wales who would object to the war on both religious and socialist grounds. Germany was extolled as the birthplace of the Protestant Reformation, and nonconformists held military life in deep distrust. Labour supporters also admired the German socialist party, and the Labour movement considered the stockpiling of armaments to be a corrupt plot to benefit profiteers.

The officers of regiments such as the Royal Welch Fusiliers were drawn from the Welsh landowning class, but nine out of ten of the ordinary soldiers came from England. For the rest of the army, there were few Welsh officers, and Lord Kitchener, Lloyd George's predecessor as Minister of War, at one time had intended to scatter the Welsh among the various regiments of the army, forbidding them to speak Welsh on parade and in their billets.

It was Lloyd George who eventually convinced himself that Britain needed to take part in the war, and developed the theme, to appeal to the patriotism of the Welsh, that as the independence of Serbia and Belgium had been crushed by Germany and Austro-Hungary, it was possible to portray the war as a crusade in support of small nations, implicitly suggesting that Wales was one of them. Lloyd George persuaded the chapels that the war was a crusade and, as a result there was a sudden influx of Welsh volunteers.

Yet there is reason to believe that conscientious objectors were proportionately more numerous in Wales than in the kingdom as a whole, and Lloyd George promised that they would have a 'very hard path'. They were sentenced to hard labour which in the case of Alan's father involved stone breaking on Dartmoor in all weathers. They were also segregated in a special wing for their own safety, although this proved to be of benefit, encouraging a sense of group identity, with plenty of opportunity for political discussion.

Their experiences were recorded in *Y Deyrnas* [Kingdom], the monthly magazine of the Welsh pacifists, whose point of view, as the war dragged on, became increasingly acceptable in radical and nonconformist circles in Wales.

At the same time, unrest was increasing among the miners of the south Wales coalfield. This sprang not so much from criticism of the war itself, as from the belief that the miners' willingness to respond positively to the demands of the government was being exploited by the coalmine owners.

Alan's father was a colliery checkweigher. There were two checkweighers in every colliery, one representing the colliers and what they were earning per shift, and one to represent the employers. The drams of coal carried chalk marks to identify the miner who had loaded it, and this was checked by the employers' representative.

Alan's father, like most checkweighers, was heavily involved in the South Wales Miners Federation (later the NUM), assisting miners in compensation cases. He became the first secretary of the largely union-funded local hospital, and visited the Soviet Union with the federation in 1938. Alan has donated, for posterity, his father's diary of this Soviet visit to the South Wales Miners Library in Swansea University, set up some 20 years ago by Dr Hywel Francis, MP for Aberavon.

The period after the First World War was a time of continual industrial unrest and argument over wage structures. The anthracite area in the western part of the south Wales coalfield had been developed by a number of small coalmine owners. However, after the war, most of the pits came into the possession of two large combines. As the new owners wanted unrestricted control, and the workers were determined to retain their traditional rights, conflict was inevitable.

The most important traditional right was the seniority rule: last in, first out. The refusal of the manager of the Number One Pit, Ammanford, to observe the rule was the main cause of the strike which spread through the anthracite coalfield in midsummer 1925. There was a great deal of violence, and Ammanford was controlled by the strike committee for ten days. After the disturbances, 198 miners were prosecuted, 58 of them imprisoned.

Alan's father was among those imprisoned, for picketing outside Crynant Colliery in the Neath valley, where the Amman Valley miners had marched in protest against blackleg labour. He spent three months in Swansea jail. He returned home a local hero.

The strike lasted almost two months, and the agreement which ended it did preserve the seniority rule.

The vast majority of the anthracite miners were Welsh speakers, and loyal to the chapel, so many were actually less militant than their fellow steam-coal miners in other districts. But John Davies concludes his account by suggesting that the Ammanford miners were greatly radicalised by the troubles of 1925.

Alan's father was a well-known and respected unionist, and when he died of emphysema at the young age of 45 in 1940, the funeral cortège extended for more than half a mile.

Alan partly inherited his father's radicalism. After his Bethesda preacher, who he admired greatly, was replaced by an evangelical 'Bible basher', Alan, like his father, became a secular atheist. And while a student at Aberystwyth he also became active in the Socialist Society.

The society was affiliated to the communist-led International Union of Students. After the invasion of Czechoslovakia in 1947, the society broke off its affiliation and reformed as the Labour Club, part of the National Association of Labour Students Organisation (NALSO). Alan, during his teacher training year, became NALSO's Welsh regional representative and organiser.

His radicalism essentially focused on two causes: CND (he attended all the Aldermaston marches) and the championing of comprehensive schooling.

Two years of National Service prevented Alan from continuing his political interests, although later, as a family man in south London he did become involved to a degree in local party politics.

Alan, again like his father, had a fairly ambivalent attitude towards the armed forces, which frequently found expression in his behaviour during National Service. All soldiers were required to salute officers they passed in the street, and Alan would always perform this task in such a theatrical manner that it verged on the disrespectful. For his last six weeks of National Service he was demoted from sergeant and 'returned to unit', following a verbal altercation with a military policeman.

Alan's son, Huw, appears also to exhibit a degree of radicalism, but in an altogether different direction. Huw was a free spirit, a hippy, a restless wanderer, doing all things that are fashionable in the alternative society. And he believed his parents to be guilty of a most serious offence, bringing him up in such a very, very anglicised suburban setting.

He obtained a degree in maths, and was trained as a computer programmer by Esso. In his mid twenties he became a freelance IT engineer. Contract work, as well as being exceptionally lucrative, also gave him the freedom to alternate his projects with travelling the world. It eventually became more offensive to be doing any work at all, and he lived for the time when a contract came to an end.

Now in his mid fifties, he has ceased travelling, and settled in Bridport, becoming quite non-political, not even taking a daily newspaper.

His earlier travels however had taken him to Canada, including a tree plantation in the wilds of Alberta, and to Mexico, where he fell in love. He was a firm believer in the role of language in helping to integrate into a community and learnt French while living in Montreal, and also became a fluent Spanish speaker while in Mexico.

At one stage he became entranced by Buddhism, becoming a novice monk in, of all places, Hemel Hempstead. On the verge of taking his vows, he was distracted again by his love of a female visitor who had come to practise meditation at the monastery. The love affair didn't however last.

Huw also spent time at a famous hippy commune in

Cwm Du, near Llandeilo, not that far from Alan's home in Glanaman. The open air life in a tepee was idyllic, and Huw was popular, especially loved by the children of the families in the commune.

But winter was a different matter; 'pissing with rain, and dark by four in the afternoon'. This drove Huw to spend time at the family home in Glanaman. Alan always knew when he had been in the house from the smells of wood smoke and his lifestyle. Huw eventually gave up on Cwm Du, and spent two years living in Glanaman.

During this period he even attempted to learn Welsh. Despite being an excellent linguist, familiar with Latin and Greek as well as French and Spanish, Welsh proved a problem. The 'formal register' taught in Welsh classes didn't prepare him for the 'cwm vernacular' of pub and street conversation. So he ended up never really feeling fully Welsh, language being far more important to a sense of Welshness in Glanaman when compared to Llanelli.

# 4

# Welsh Language

IN THE INDUSTRIAL and population expansion of south Wales in the late 19th and early 20th century, when there was large-scale immigration from England, most of the migrants to these western valleys were still Welsh speakers from rural Carmarthenshire and Cardiganshire. And in recent decades, English immigrants in search of second homes or alternative lifestyles have favoured other more rural parts of south, mid and north Wales. Thus, even in the 2001 census, the Amman Valley was reported as being 85 per cent Welsh speaking.

Alan's grandmother had been virtually a monoglot Welsh speaker. Her English was halting, and she wasn't comfortable with it in prolonged conversation.

During Alan's childhood, Welsh was the language of the home and the street, but without any official status, gave way to English in business and government. Alan's early perceptions of the county town of Carmarthen were of a professional population for whom the speaking of English was a badge of social status, spoken with 'a twang' with rounded vowels and no dropped aitches.

Interestingly, his father, when holding meetings with miners and trade unionists at the house, would begin by talking socially in Welsh in the kitchen, and then retire to the parlour to conduct their business in English.

Alan had a good command of Welsh, both from home and chapel, but when faced with a choice of French or Welsh after his first year in secondary school, was encouraged by his mother and the rest of the family to stay with French. It was considered that he could already speak Welsh, and French would be of more use in the wider world. And half the family were, in any case, French teachers.

For some reason the Welsh have no need to expand Welsh horizons, and introduce their way of life to the rest of the world. The Welsh language is merely something they use at home. It is just part of their way of life, but of no use elsewhere. Until recently, it had no part to play in daily business or government.

The result is that Alan considers his Welsh, like many of his peers, to be 90 per cent vernacular. And he believes, partly as a result of its lack of status in earlier years, and the minimal interest in studying Welsh academically, that the gap between the vernacular and formal register of Welsh is greater than with other languages. Although, when teaching in south London, Alan also appreciated the wide gap between cockney and the Queen's English.

Some years ago in the bowls club, Alan had a discussion about the Welsh language with an older London Welsh supporter from Maesteg, whom I recall traditionally always wore a suit and tie, even for a rugby match. The old guy had learnt 'book' Welsh and claimed he would have given his right arm to speak fluent vernacular Welsh. Alan, on the other hand, would like to speak good enough Welsh to appear on television. (At least as long as he'd had a haircut.) But he actually claims to find the Welsh spoken by the newsreaders on S4C difficult to understand.

Formal Welsh can also be rejected by more colloquial speakers. In the Half Moon pub in Glanaman, on his frequent trips 'home', Alan speaks of his fellow drinkers being derogatory, using the local Amman Valley vernacular Welsh *sians* (ostentatious), if someone introduces more formal Welsh into the conversation. There is some sense of formal Welsh being the preserve of the middle classes.

Sadly, vernacular Welsh is more prone to adopt anglicised words than formal Welsh. On rugby broadcasts, the referee is *y dyfarnwr;* in the pub he is *y reffari.* On television a try is *cais,* in the pub it is *trei,* although paradoxically Welsh spelling and rules of mutation are still applied: 'try' becomes *trei* becomes *y drei.*

It was the gap between the 'formal register' of his Welsh classes and the vernacular conversations of the Half Moon that gave Alan's son, Huw, his problems with Welsh. He was always having to stop and think before speaking, by which time someone else had made the same point.

Welsh has now acquired some equality, at least in local government. But one of the Half Moon drinkers, and fellow Côr Dyffryn Aman chorister, who is also a high-ranking county council official, has spoken to Alan of the difficulties he encounters adjusting his formal workplace Welsh to the requirements of the pub environment.

A fellow student of Alan's, Gwyn Alfred Williams (known as 'Gwyn Alpha' because he was always getting firsts for his essays, later becoming professor of history at Aberystwyth), had spoken Welsh in childhood but had let it fall into disuse, feeling it wasn't needed on an everyday basis.

However, on attending the funeral of Dai Francis (a former prominent member of the NUM, and father of Hywel Francis, MP for Aberavon), Gwyn had been struck by how many of the NUM members and ex-miners present were fluent Welsh speakers.

And travelling to the funeral on the bus from Aberystwyth, the miner in the next seat turned and asked: *'Wyt ti'n Gymro?'* ('Are you a Welsh speaker?'). Gwyn was ashamed to say 'no'.

He resolved to relearn Welsh, and eventually even gave lectures in Welsh. Yet, chatting with Alan in a pub after one lecture, he still couldn't handle the language of the vernacular.

What hope is there of Welsh being spoken by future generations and Welsh exiles?

Alan was disappointed recently, when watching the Public School Rugby Sevens at Roehampton, to hear fluent Welsh-speaking pupils from Ysgol y Strade, Llanelli, conversing in

English on the touchline. This is also true of youngsters drinking in the Half Moon, and is a regular bone of contention among the 'oldies' in the pub. English has become the fashionable language of choice for younger people.

In Alan's schooldays, while English was the language of the classroom, Welsh had been the language of the playground. And while the rapid growth of Welsh-medium primary and secondary schools has seen a massive increase in classroom Welsh, we have today the reverse scenario of English being the language of the playground.

However, this is not necessarily encouraged by the establishment. In previous centuries, Welsh was forbidden in the playground, with those caught speaking Welsh being forced to wear a wooden collar, 'the Welsh Not'. Linden, a fellow chorister of Alan's and a teacher of English at Welsh-medium school Ysgol Gŵyr (previously Gowerton Grammar School) now claims that pupils from more anglicised Swansea are criticised by staff if caught speaking English.

Attendance at Welsh-medium schools has become very desirable for the children of middle class and professional families, whose parents perceive career and cultural advantages for their children in being able to speak, read and write in Welsh. Alan points out that, in the Amman Valley, aspirational parents often choose the Welsh-medium school in Ystalyfera in the next valley in preference to the local Amman Valley Comprehensive, despite the 12-mile bus journey. Such schools have also achieved huge impact and status in more English-speaking areas such as Pontypridd, Bridgend and the capital city, Cardiff.

For a Welsh exile however the situation is more difficult. Alan speaks Welsh, and has strong links with his home village of Glanaman, but like myself, he has spent his professional life in London, and also married an English girl.

In addition, he has not fostered any strong Welsh links in the capital. Being an atheist, he did not find a haven in the London Welsh chapel community, although his father's sister and her husband, Auntie May and Uncle Billy, were very involved with the Methodist Chapel in Walham Green, Fulham. They used to tell him about the chapel and their part in the London Welsh cultural activities, including sport, socialising and even learning a little Welsh. But Alan was put off by the way Billy used to use the annual *Adroddiad* [Report] to name and shame members who didn't contribute enough to chapel funds. 'A true blue Cardi', according to Alan.

Alan's children follow the family tradition of being good linguists. His daughter, Kathryn, has a degree in French and Russian. But none has any interest in the Welsh language. They don't go down to Wales often enough, and they have no other opportunity to speak it. So Alan didn't feel it was appropriate to be 'stuffing Welsh down their throats'. To repeat a previous observation, the Welsh it seems have no desire to impose their culture on others. They just want the freedom to carry on with their own way of life.

All Alan's children are, however, fanatical Welsh rugby fans.

# 5

# Welsh Nationalism

THE STRONG LIBERAL and radical tendencies of the Welsh, the belief in equal opportunity for all men, has seldom translated itself into a drive for their own independence.

Travel writer, Jan Morris, observed in her book *Wales: Epic Views of a Small Country*, that 'at its best, the radical instinct of the Welsh runs deeper than nationalism or economics, and is concerned in all its manifestations with the human condition itself. It is a profound, if intermittent feeling for dignity, embedded in the nature of the Welsh tradition – dignity in private life, dignity in nationhood.'

She goes on to say that 'the Welsh have seldom suffered from national ambition, only national grievance'.

Thus socialism became radicalism only when the establishment in Westminster was seen as the enemy. John Davies writes: 'The subjection of the Welsh as a nation was interwoven with their subjection as peasants or industrial workers, and that salvation would not come unless they challenged the power structures which enslaved them.'

The nonconformist religions also stressed the rights of individuals not communities, and only became radical when confronted by the need to disestablish the Welsh church and sever its connection with the Church of England. But in the broader context, nonconformist beliefs were seen as only being hindered by focusing just on Wales.

Another strand of Welsh nationalism was of course the preservation of the Welsh language. In 1850, two out of every three spoke Welsh, many of them only Welsh. Strangely, the industrial developments of the second half of the 19th century had both a positive and negative effect on this situation. On the one hand, industry offered a livelihood to a substantial population, including many rural workers, who would otherwise have emigrated. But the industrialisation of south Wales also involved considerable immigration, and English was still the language of business and government. Thus Welsh wasn't essential to daily existence.

The survival of the language is however essential for the continuation of a language-based Welsh culture. So by the late 1990s, every schoolchild in Wales had learnt something of the Welsh language.

John Davies explores the reasons why Welsh nationalism didn't develop in the early part of the 20th century, as it did in other, what he calls 'non-historic nations', such as Czechoslovakia and Slovenia. One reason he feels why nationhood happened in these countries and not in Wales, is that these eastern European nations had strong intellectual foundations based on their universities, and a strong scholarly interest in traditions. Welsh Anglicans, on the other hand, looked to English universities, from which Welsh universities also initially derived their degrees. Welsh nonconformists and socialists in parallel were less well-educated and less concerned with nationalism.

John Davies goes on to say that while 'consciousness of Welsh nationality was deeply rooted, the notion that there should be political structures which would give expression to this consciousness was not put forward until the second half of the 19th century... most obvious among those who had experience outside Wales'.

Is this why I am more nationalistic than my friends who stayed at home? In some ways, Welshness is mostly encouraged when spending time with fellow exiles for the express purpose of preserving the culture, rather than living everyday life in Wales itself. If I hadn't lived in England, would I have made the effort to learn Welsh (in Wales I might have felt embarrassed to speak to fluent Welsh speakers), and would I have bothered to try to join a choir?

Nationhood has not always been something that has bothered the indigenous population of Wales itself. American Pamela Petro paints a more abstract picture of what it means to be Welsh: 'Welshness has been a secular construction, consciously fashioned by English and Welsh speakers alike, out of song, grit, pride in origins however humble, a profound respect for difference, and beer. Add to that a streak of wounded defiance directed more practically at the English government, plus an unreined and unapologetic joy in anything the least bit interesting.'

This thesis is echoed by John Winterson Richards in his *Xenophobe's Guide to the Welsh*: 'A Welshman's accent in English is a poor guide to whether or not he speaks Welsh. Even the ability to speak Welsh is of itself a poor measure of Welshness. So is living in Wales, or having Welsh relatives. Welshness is an attitude of mind – sometimes psychopathic, often generous, usually friendly, and always passionate.'

And according to Jan Morris, Wales '... is not just a country on the map, or even in the mind; it is a country of the heart, and all of us have some small country there.'

# 6

# English Residence

THE CONTINUITY OF both Alan's Welshness and socialism was disrupted by National Service. This he spent as part of the Royal Army Educational Corp, based in Catterick, in North Yorkshire. It was his duty to broaden the education of staff across all army units, and as the various unit commanders resented releasing their staff, he had a lot of time on his hands, mainly spent enjoyably reading in the camp's excellent library.

Social life was also good, and it was here he met, Diane, a local girl who eventually became his wife.

Following his previously mentioned altercation with the military policeman, he was stripped of his sergeant's stripes, and ignominiously returned to unit, which meant the Educational Corps in Beaconsfield, Bucks.

Here he spent the last six weeks of his army life. In readiness for his demob, Diane joined him from Yorkshire, and Alan took time off to apply to London County Council for a probationary teaching post. The sergeant major refused to grant him leave, but was overruled by the unit's commanding officer. So the sergeant major, taking his revenge, ensured that Alan was every day allocated the worst chore, effectively 'cleaning the bogs'. Not a very auspicious end to Alan's army career.

Alan finally obtained a teaching post in a south London secondary modern school, and settled in Clapham Junction, familiar to Alan as the home of his father's sister. He continued to take the *Western Mail* to keep an eye out for teaching posts 'back home', but this brought little success. So he stayed put in south-west London, moving from one rented accommodation to another, until, after three years, he took out a mortgage on a maisonette in Mitcham.

After 15 years teaching in a LCC school in Surrey, Alan took a year's secondment to take a diploma of education at the London Institute, specialising in the history of education and educational psychology. Qualifying with distinction, he was successful in obtaining a lectureship at a teachers' training college in Englefield Green in Surrey in 1968, applying the psychology of education to the practice of teaching.

Shoreditch College, as it was called, was actually a training college for craft and design teachers. Alan's craft knowledge was non-existent, but this wasn't essential. Alan felt he could impart the process of education irrespective of the subject matter being taught.

It was an all-male establishment with horseplay in abundance, a generally anti-cultural ethos, and great scepticism about the value of educational theory and the 'education lecturers with their jargon'.

However this proved the perfect setting for Alan to hone his skills as a sympathetic lecturer and public speaker par excellence, using stories to illustrate key principles, in the true manner of the successful nonconformist minister, 'Davies Bethel', he had first encountered in the chapels of his youth.

In his lectures Alan quoted the writings of Jean Piaget, the Swiss philosopher and natural scientist, focusing on their relevance to teaching.

Piaget was originally a biologist, but moved on to study the development of child understanding. He examined the way we think as we develop, from earliest childhood to mature adolescence, arguing that some of the features of childhood thinking, in fact, persist into adulthood, in particular illogical and contradictory thoughts.

Always looking for ways to illustrate his concepts with examples, Alan talked of his seven-year-old daughter Judith, whispering in his ear one day that she didn't believe in God. Alan questioned why she was whispering. 'In case he hears me,' she replied.

Alan's next move, in 1972, was to Garnett College, one of the few colleges in the UK where further education lecturers, as opposed to teachers, were trained. One of his first students, later to become a colleague, was Jim 'Third Verse' Jenkins of bowls club fame. Jim recalls this guy coming to the lectern, moving it powerfully back and forth in the manner of a Welsh preacher, with a distinguished face like the poet R S Thomas, and a Georgie Best 1970s haircut.

Alan began speaking: 'May I welcome you to Garnett College, a particularly warm welcome if you're Welsh, and if you're Welsh-speaking please come round for a chat afterwards.' (And some did, allegedly.)

Jim speaks of a student, a craft teacher, complaining about lecturers who looked down on craft teachers, *telling* them how to teach, and comparing these to Alan, who 'knew his onions, treated us with respect, and *showed* us how to teach'.

This reflects Alan's strong support for Carl Rogers, an influential American psychologist and one of the founders of the humanistic approach to psychology. This focused on a so-called 'person-centred' therapy, encouraging individuals to perceive problems within the context of their own experiences, desires and value systems. 'Not how can I treat or cure, but how can I provide a relationship which this person may use for his own personal growth.' (Carl Rogers)

Applied to education this meant the student learning for him or herself ('student-centred learning') and not just to meet criteria set by the teacher. This reflects on Alan's early experiences teaching in a secondary modern school in Balham. Here he came to realise that what really matters is what matters to the pupil. Hence the early school leavers in Form 4X had no interest in the foreign policies of Castlereagh or Canning, but they could be induced to take an interest in the General Strike or First World War experiences as described in Robert Graves's book *Goodbye to All That*.

Carl Rogers went on to talk about 'the good life' achieved by individuals having 'a growing openness to experience' ('the fully functioning person').

An important idea of Carl Rogers was the link between 'psychological safety' and 'psychological freedom'. Rogers argued that if we create a 'climate of safety' for ourselves and our students, we are more likely to take risks with ideas, to try things, and not to be cramped by fears of failure. These qualities will create self-confidence and enjoyment of learning for its own sake.

Such thoughts seem to me to bear a striking resemblance to Jan Morris's description of Welshness as being 'concerned with the human condition'. Could Carl Rogers be yet another American with a hidden Welsh ancestry?

Alan's promotion to principal lecturer in 1975 involved going around all the different faculties encouraging the application of teaching theory to practice. Alan's main aim was to deal with the mismatch between theory and practice.

It was exactly the kind of role in which Alan revelled, being a catalyst for stimulating thought and action, without having to bother with a load of administration, committee meetings or 'bossing' people around. Not for Alan the pressures of management, just storytelling and psychologising.

How even more Welsh!

# 7

# Home to the Valley

IN SIMILAR CIRCUMSTANCES to myself, it was the availability of work which resulted in Alan settling in London, but whereas I had found the time as a bachelor boy in the 1960s to seek out what there was of Welsh society in London, Alan was more preoccupied with being a family man in the more austere 1950s, eventually with three children, living in a one-room shoe box, and struggling financially to handle the high rents on a teacher's salary.

Shoreditch College in fact had relocated to Englefield Green in Surrey, which was both a long 40-mile round car journey each day for Alan, but also six miles outside the area which qualified for a London salary weighting.

Glanaman was visited only once or twice a year, and many of his school friends like himself had moved away. So gradually Alan lost touch with his roots.

He also resisted the temptation to force Welshness down his children's throats, although all three showed Welsh traits in their chosen lives, Huw with his radicalism, Kathryn becoming involved in social care and Judith becoming a primary school teacher.

Alan even played rugby for the local Streatham team rather than the more demanding London Welsh. Only available for home games when younger, he actually played for Streatham Occasionals, made up either of 40/50-year-old has-beens or beginners with limited aptitude. He was a PE teacher at the time, so was probably the fittest man in the team, scoring a load of tries in the last ten to fifteen minutes of games, when everyone else was knackered. As the star player, I wonder if he had his hair cut before every match?

Subsequently, with more time on his hands, he played for Merton Rugby Club's first XV for more than a decade, not retiring until he was 36. He claims he could never have carried on for this length of time if he had continued living in Glanaman where the rugby was far too competitive and dirty for a natural physical coward like himself.

Amazingly Alan became the only survivor from among the surprisingly few offspring produced by his mother and her four siblings, and his father and his four siblings. So about a quarter of a century ago, in 1983, he inherited his great-grandfather's house in The Square, Glanaman. And his Welsh identity was re-established with far more frequent trips 'home'.

The Square is the centre of the village, the area where the post office, most of the shops, and the local community centre are located. So on leaving the house he would always meet lots of people, and Welsh-speaking people. It could often take him half an hour to get to the post office and back, Alan being Alan.

He has become a resident 'belonger' to the Amman Valley community (*perthyn*: 'to belong' as we say in Welsh). He has even become president of the local Amman Valley Choir, Côr Dyffryn Aman, and a regular in the Half Moon.

In London, now that his rugby playing days were over, he took to watching London Welsh with his colleague and former student, Jim Jenkins. One afternoon they were joined on the touchline by Wilbur and Alan Cole from Seaside, Llanelli, whom they invited back to the clubhouse for a drink. Wilbur and Alan Cole gave them a look. 'We don't drink there, but there,' said Wilbur, pointing at what looked like a green garden shed behind the tennis courts, which we have all now come to love as the Mid Surrey Bowls Club.

Alan soon befriended fellow Welsh speaker and chief pitcher of hymns, Dai Heart Attack, and is now a fully fledged, card-carrying 'deacon'. He can also be heard before most home matches deep in conversation with the Welsh-speaking fraternity in The Shaftesbury in Richmond, particularly Dai Pugh, a fellow Amman Valley exile and West London dairyman, who rivals even Aesop as a storyteller.

At home Alan continues to encourage his granddaughter Sophie in the ways of the Welsh, singing Welsh lullabies ('Ar Lan y Môr') and ditties ('Oes Gafr Eto') to her at bedtime. She is also learning Welsh via the internet, apparently at a far more rapid rate than yours truly.

Every December I receive Alan's Welsh-language, dragon-adorned Christmas card, designed by Sophie on her PC. Alan is particularly pleased that, as a result of the invention of the postcode, he can send these cards to Wales bearing Welsh-language addresses, without giving the Royal Mail any sleepless nights.

He is not, however, about to make a permanent move back to Wales. The way of life typified by the Half Moon and the Amman United Rugby Club is both totally male-dominated and Welsh-speaking, neither of which, to be fair, is particularly welcoming to an English wife.

Jan Morris also once proffered the opinion that 'by and large, the London Welsh are as devoted to Wales as anyone, except that, in the wisdom of their worldliness, they prefer to live well away from the place'.

But, for Alan, trips 'home' have become an essential and regular contributor to the preservation of his Welshness.

And the 40-strong Amman Valley Choir demonstrated the regard with which they hold their president by travelling all the way up from Glanaman to attend, along with 50 others, a surprise 80th birthday party for Alan held, where else, but the bowls club.

The party was kept a secret by announcing that on the said weekend, the choir would be singing at the awards ceremony of the World Coracle Racing Championships in Llangollen (codenamed Operation Coracle). Everyone crossed their fingers that Alan had no interest in coracle racing, or a weekend away in Llangollen with the boys.

In the event the surprise worked perfectly. Alan was led to believe he was just having a quiet birthday drink with a few of us in the Shaftesbury and was then persuaded to visit the bowls club where he was greeted by a chorus of 'Penblwydd Hapus' from the assembled gathering which included both the choir and 50 other friends from London Welsh.

The choir's subsequent half-hour rendering of hymns and songs even included 'Ar Lan y Môr' and 'Oes Gafr Eto', much to the delight of granddaughter Sophie.

# A 'Gog' Perspective

**Richard Williams**

**David Davies**

Richard Williams is a 54-year-old North Walian (*Gog*) and fellow Welsh learner (*dysgwr Cymraeg)* at the London Welsh Centre (*Canolfan Cymru Llundain)* in Gray's Inn Road. He no longer needs to attend classes, his Welsh being far superior to mine, and is now part of the *Cylch Siarad* (Welsh speakers circle) which meets in the bar each week to converse only in Welsh; that is, until the learners such as myself join them after classes and nudge the conversation back to English as a result of our inadequacies in the mother tongue.

Richard is a reader in immunology at Imperial College, London, and has spent the last 20-odd years researching the intricacies of the immune system and developing new treatments for auto-immune diseases.

He hails originally from Llanfaelog, a rural district close to the north-west coast of Anglesey, comprising the villages of Llanfaelog, Rhosneigr, Bryn Du and Pencarnisiog.

Cynics might protest that Richard is my token Gog in this series of biographies, but it is important to cover attitudes from different parts of the country, and it has proved interesting to note how similar his emotions and experiences have been to my south-west Wales experience.

Despite being brought up in north rather than south Wales, in the 1960s as opposed to the 1950s, and in a much more rural environment than Llanelli, Richard, like myself, remembers his childhood for its sense of friendliness and community, in a region with a similar mix of Welsh-speaking (Pencarnisiog) and non-Welsh-speaking areas (the seaside village of Rhosneigr with its holiday homes) where a feeling was perpetuated that you needed to speak English rather than Welsh to get on in this world.

\*

David (Dafydd) Davies, another Welsh learner, was born in Essex, but with a Welsh father who also hailed from north Wales, from a tenant farm in Pistyll on the Llŷn peninsula.

The area suffered greatly during the 1930s Depression, and Dafydd's father was forced to seek work in London, the farm providing insufficient livelihood to support himself in addition to his parents and three brothers.

Gwynedd is the heartland of the Welsh language, so the family were monoglot Welsh speakers, and Dafydd's dad arrived in London not speaking a word of English. Dafydd, despite growing up in an isolated rural part of Essex, with little Welsh contact apart from his father's family in north Wales, has never seen himself as anything other than Welsh, and like me is now in his retirement making time to improve his understanding of the Welsh language.

# Richard Williams

1

# Welsh Village Life

J GERAINT JENKINS wrote, for the World Conference on Records: Preserving our Heritage, 1980, about 'Life and Traditions in Rural Wales', claiming that 'the study of any area which has had a long history of human settlement shows quite clearly that the cultural landscape contains many elements besides those associated with the present-day life of the inhabitants. The cultural landscape of such an area has been compared with an ancient manuscript that has been written over on several occasions.'

Thus Richard's perceptions of life in Wales being friendlier with a greater sense of community, are not only shared by the other Welsh exiles whose stories are presented in this book, but have their foundations in the history of Wales as far back as the Middle Ages.

The structure of Welsh villages is very different to the romanticised image of the English village with its lord of the manor, village green, community hall, church and pub.

The Wales of the Middle Ages, according to J Geraint Jenkins, involved:

> ... a semi-nomadic people with strong tribal affinities, practising a pastoral economy. From the eleventh century the numerous Welsh princes attempted to settle these nomadic pastoralists in permanent homesteads. The unit of landholding in medieval Wales was that of a *gwely* [bed], which was an association of

people bound together by blood relationship. The position of the individual within the *gwely* depended not on his contract but on consanguinity [having the same ancestor]... As time progressed, the existing land was subdivided among the kin group, for on the death of a head of family his wealth did not descend to his eldest son but was divided equally among all his sons and, after their day, among the grandsons... The continued subdivision of property meant smaller and more scattered holdings... [a pattern of settlement which] is often quite recognisable in rural Wales today.

In addition peasant families would set up a *tŷ unnos* (one-night house) on the previously unoccupied (common) land: 'The custom was that if a house of turf was built in a single night and smoke was seen emanating from the chimney at dawn, then the occupier of that temporary dwelling had a legal right to the homestead. An axe thrown from the house marked the extent of an enclosure around the homestead.'

According to John Davies in *A History of Wales*, the Welsh king, Hywel Dda (Howell the Good) systemised these legal customs that had developed over the centuries. The emphasis was on reconciliation between kinship groups rather than keeping order through punishment. Key elements were mercy, commonsense and respect for women and children. Much of the benefits of these laws were unfortunately lost with the demise of Welsh independence under Edward I.

To return to J Geraint Jenkins:

In medieval Welsh society the law of civil obligation meant that... at harvest time... cooperation was very widely practised, and the individual farmer considered it his duty to help his neighbour, knowing that this favour would be repaid when the need arose.

Strangers who visit parts of rural Wales are often impressed by the great deal of kindness, hospitality, and welcome they receive. This again is but a reflection of the tribal past and owes its origin to the keeping of an open house for those in need.

Although in areas of dispersed settlement no village as such may be found, the very way of life and the whole social atmosphere... are such, that a kind of family feeling, an idea of common destiny... exist between each family and the whole locality. Rural Wales, the land of local cultures, supports a society as tribal in its organisation today as that of the early inhabitants described in the Welsh laws.

The relative isolation... and the distribution of the homesteads... have tended to emphasise the individuality of character. When folk foregathered, it was not on the village green... or in the village tavern... as in England, but around the hearth of the individual farmstead... [and] much of the informality of the hearth has been transferred to the services of the local places of worship and to concerts held in the parish halls... The latter still possess much of the informality of the traditional Welsh *noson lawen* [literally "merry evening"] which was once commonly conducted in the farm kitchen.

The other distinguishing aspect of the medieval Welsh economy was its emphasis on animal husbandry rather than cereal cultivation. Livestock farming never needed the elaborate equipment of arable farming. This, plus the widespread distribution of homesteads, meant that specialised craftsmen, so common in English villages, were a rarity in Wales.

Again according to J Geraint Jenkins:

As in peasant societies the world over, a great deal of the equipment was made by the farmers themselves, rather than by craftsmen... Farmers often showed considerable artistry in their work... [and] it was this tradition that gave Wales its lovespoons... products of an upland peasantry that lived in isolation.

[However] in every community there were always one or two people who were more competent than others. In the self-sufficient rural neighbourhood, the specialised craftsman, whether full or part-time, was an integral member of society. If a community did not possess all the artisans necessary for its survival, then the rural areas always possessed their groups of itinerant craftsmen.

But things have changed in rural Wales; for since 1939 the agricultural economy has been completely transformed... One of the most significant social changes which came as a result

of technological improvement was the complete destruction
of the neighbourhood group with its intimacy of association
and cooperative organisation. Today each farm tends to be an
economic unit, almost completely independent of its neighbours.

As a result of the decline of rural industry the countryside has
lost something more than economic units producing essential
goods; it has also lost an important avenue of expression, for in
the social history of the countryside the importance of the craft
workshop as a meeting place for the rural community cannot be
overestimated. In many cases the cobbler's shop, the smithy, and
the carpenter's yard were social centres where problems were
discussed, where argument was rife, and where wit of the highest
level was the order of the day.

Some of this spirit must still have lived on in the rural Wales of
Richard's 1960s childhood.

His grandfather was the local vet and farrier. His father also
trained as a vet at college in Liverpool where he met his wife-
to-be, Richard's mother. He then returned to manage the farm
lands while Richard's mother handled the veterinary practice.

The local villages had no focal point; there was no village
hall, few shops, even less today, and a very small, old fashioned
pub, which only sold whisky or ale direct from the barrel. And
Richard's memories of Welsh friendliness mainly emanated
from accompanying his father or mother in their work.

He observes that in Wales people are generally happy to
greet another human being without thinking 'What's he after?'
– unlike in London, where people 'are always immediately
suspicious'.

'People were always speaking to people they didn't know,'
and he recalls the family setting up a home in an out-house
for a local tramp who had come to the end of his days as a
traveller.

Such values even persist today. George Monbiot talks in
*The Guardian* of being told by Elfyn Llwyd, Plaid Cymru MP
for Dwyfor Meirionnydd, of a local farm whose tenants were

about to be evicted because the farmer had been killed in an accident. The neighbouring farmers clubbed together and told the landlord they would look after the husbandry until the oldest boy turned 18.

Elfyd Llwyd concluded: 'Perhaps it's a result of living in a sparsely populated area. We help each other because we know each other... Traditionally Welsh people belong to the left. There's a deep and ingrained sense of fair play. They want to see people being looked after. The University of Bangor was built on donations from quarrymen, earning a pittance because they wanted a better future for their children.'

Richard does admit that this difference in attitude compared to his present London abode could be the function of a rural environment compared to that of a big city, although he has also found urban Wales very welcoming, an opinion formed, unprompted I emphasise, while on holiday in Llanelli last summer. Richard observed that 'it's a really nice place; walking along, everyone would say hello to you'.

Richard's memories of his Anglesey childhood are similarly all about friendliness.

## 2

# Getting On and Getting Out

THE WEST COAST of Anglesey is not a particularly rich area, and J Geraint Jenkins talks of Newborough, a little further south of Richard's home village, being described by a nineteenth-century traveller as:

> ... the most miserable spot in Anglesey... with men eking out a living on poor agricultural land that was constantly under threat from advancing sea dunes. The women were concerned with weaving marram grass, about the only vegetation that could grow on the sand dunes, and although this craft was undoubtedly started so as to provide essentials for the local community itself, in time it developed into a major craft industry. The marram grass products of Newborough were sold throughout Gwynedd, and the practice of weaving meant the difference between starvation and existence to a poverty-stricken community.

If you had land, according to Richard, you were fine, but people were really scared of poverty. His father was always speaking about the poverty he had witnessed growing up in the Depression of the 1930s, developing the belief that 'to do well, you had to get out' and to achieve this he believed in giving his offspring a 'better education' which in his eyes meant one that was middle class and predominantly English. In this he was supported by Richard's mother who was English with a parson for a father. She was also obviously well educated as it must have been quite revolutionary at the time for a woman to qualify as a vet.

Richard's father had been unable to speak English before

going to primary school, but in order to take over the veterinary business it was felt that he should receive the best possible education, firstly by attending boarding school and subsequently by receiving formal training as a vet.

Richard also remembers frequently speaking Welsh before going to primary school, especially to Glyn, a first language Welsh speaker who lived next door. But the decision was then taken to send Richard and his siblings to the predominantly English-speaking primary school in the holiday village of Rhosneigr, rather than to the Welsh-language school in Pencarnisiog.

The family also worshipped at a local Anglican church. There were services in both English and Welsh, but the family only attended the former.

Then following in their father's footsteps, all the children, brothers and sisters, were sent to boarding school.

Richard himself became very homesick. This was the first time in his life he was made aware of class distinction. He had been brought up in an environment where everyone was part of the same community. Some were richer than others, but there was no conscious distinction between people; no family was better than another.

Boarding school changed all that. It was not that the boys were snobbish, but they were made to feel different, distinct and separate from the local townspeople.

It was also a very unfriendly environment. There was constant name-calling, and if you spoke out everyone tried to knock you down. This made many of the children afraid to speak out and express themselves, except for the more self-confident ones. This is in sharp contrast to what Richard calls the Welsh way – from chapel, education, eisteddfodau – of promoting self-expression in all, with children encouraged to perform from an early age without fear, thus helping to lose their inhibitions. Hence the heavy presence of Welshmen in politics, music and the theatre. In Richard's view 'boarding schools for children shouldn't be allowed'.

Although in north Wales, about two thirds of the boarding school's pupils were from the north-west of England. The school was emotionally separate from its environment; they could have been in any town. There was not a single lesson on the local area. And Welsh lessons weren't available for the few Welsh-speaking boys, although they were given a single period for a while, led by the music teacher.

What drives us non-Welsh speakers to learn the language when all around tell you it's a waste of time? Richard shared some of my feelings of guilt, ashamed when addressed by Welsh speakers and unable to respond in his country's language. So while reading for a degree in agriculture at University College, Bangor, he took time out to relearn Welsh, even living in a Welsh-speaking hall of residence to improve his grasp of the language.

Richard stayed on at Bangor to complete an M.Sc. in parasitology, the study of which helps the treatment of parasitic diseases such as malaria. Then a desire to travel took over, and he forgot about Wales for a while.

# 3

# Where Next?

For Richard travel meant adventure, learning about other cultures, but also about doing something useful to improve the condition of people. In true Welsh tradition, he is very much a socialist with a small 's'.

He quite fancied South and Central America, particularly Nicaragua, which at the time had a progressive government looking to create social change, and is also a country described as a biologist's paradise given the huge variety of its natural habitat.

Then when an old friend phoned from Spain to say there was a demand there for English teachers, he thought that this might be a good opportunity to learn Spanish before embarking on his trip to the further-flung continent.

Richard liked rural Spain. Its friendliness and sense of community brought back memories of Wales. People spoke to people they didn't know, and were 'unbelievably welcoming'. Even Spanish mothers reminded him of Welsh mothers, a little over-controlling, clearly boss in their own homes.

In the end he stayed three years. He did have talks meanwhile with the Nicararaguan embassy, but the situation there became more than a little hostile as the United States gave support to the rebels in a counter-revolution. And after six months in Spain he also met his future wife, a Spanish girl named Alicia.

The need to develop his career eventually meant a return to the UK, with Alicia joining him once he had settled into a job.

Richard's first post was as a lab technician. He went on to

complete a Ph.D. in immunology, and after further positions in Cambridge and London, he eventually became a senior lecturer at the Kennedy Institute for Rheumatoid Arthritis, which had merged with the Imperial College School of Medicine in 1997.

Richard and Alicia are now married with two boys, Thomas, aged 16, and Joseph, 13. Richard talks of the tradition in Spain, that wherever you are born, that is your nationality. Your family might be from Andalucia, but if you are born in Barcelona then you are Catalan. He sees this as an excellent model for modern society, because it means that children feel part of the community in which they are raised. So his sons, born in London, are Londoners.

Marcel Theroux, born in Uganda of an American father and English mother, puts the case more forcefully in a *Guardian* article describing his confusion over his own nationality on the eve of the USA v England World Cup football match: 'It has always seemed obvious to me that nationality is a fiction, anyway. The nation state is a bogus construct: our real ties are with families and neighbourhoods. My children are Anglo-Welsh-Americans of French-Canadian and Italian extraction. But, basically, they're from Tooting.'

Richard's sons have been brought up to speak both Spanish and English at home, so to introduce them to Welsh in addition, Richard thought, was too much of a burden. But eldest son Thomas likes Wales, and only recently came home proudly displaying a daffodil badge in his lapel, because 'it is Welsh'. And younger son, Joseph, is even more 'mad on Wales'. He wants to learn Welsh, and even supports the Scarlets.

Now every year, since turning 50, Richard feels the pull of Welsh rural life more strongly. Four of his five brothers and sisters remain in Wales, his brothers actually living in Rhosneigr with Welsh-speaking wives and children who attended Welsh-medium schools. Alicia also feels welcomed in Anglesey.

What Richard really wants is to be involved in a local

community, in a smallish village or town, close to the sea, surrounded by lovely countryside. The difficult decision is whether this will be in Spain or Wales.

# David (Dafydd) Davies

## 1

## Just Getting Out

RICHARD WILLIAMS'S FATHER believed that an English oriented education was a precursor to getting out of the region and getting on in life. Dafydd's father had no such luxury. He was uneducated, working on the farm from a very early age, deciding in his early twenties to head for London, as his family's small tenant farm in Pistyll on the Llŷn Peninsula in north Wales did not seem able to provide a sufficient livelihood to sustain his parents and three brothers as well as himself.

Dafydd however regarded him as very bright. Typical of the Welsh working classes, he read a lot, and was even a lay preacher, travelling on his bike for miles to preach, even as far as Bala, more than 40 miles from home.

Dafydd's father was born on a farm in Penrhyndeudraeth, near Porthmadog. He was in fact illegitimate and kept at home to work on the farm for much of his early years, only attending school up to the age of 12. His mother then married one of the farm workers and the three of them moved some 20-odd miles to a small tenant farm near Pistyll, on the Llŷn peninsula, later scraping together enough money to pay the rent for a larger farm of 70 acres in nearby Llithfaen. By then, Dafydd's father had three half-brothers.

It was very much subsistence farming, mainly sheep, with half a dozen cows, chickens, pigs, plus basic vegetables, and oats for cattle feed, to ensure they became self-sufficient. To raise more money, after the milking and the farm work, Dafydd's father and his stepfather would walk two miles across the hills to work in a granite quarry for the rest of the day.

While still at Pilstyll, in 1932, at the age of 24, he decided, Dick Whittington style, to seek his fortune in London. He packed a bag, was given a big send off party and a lift to the station at Pwllheli, from where he caught a train to London Euston.

On arriving at Euston, he stood alone on the platform after the crowd had departed, a monoglot Welsh speaker without a word of English, not knowing what to do next. As a policeman approached, he assumed he was about to be arrested for loitering. Amazingly the policeman was a fluent Welsh speaker, and a north Walian at that. Apparently it was the policy of the Metropolitan Police in those days to position Welsh speakers on the beat in both Euston and Paddington Stations for just such an eventuality.

The Welsh bobby took him to a Salvation Army hostel, promising to return in the morning. True to his word, the following day he introduced him to a Welsh butcher in the Euston area, who gave him a job as head cowman on his very large dairy farm in Essex. Dafydd's father slept in the straw in the loft above the barn, with cold water available from the standpipe outside the farmhouse, and use of an outside toilet. He stayed until just before the Second World War.

He then met an Irishman, George Ellis, in a pub. George had left Cork in similar circumstances to Dafydd's father, and had also cycled the 25 miles from Chelmsford just to drink in this particular pub. George claimed to be earning three times Dafydd's father's wage in a Chelmsford factory, and suggested he came to lodge with him and get a job in the factory. The factory was owned by electrical manufacturer Crompton Parkinson. Dafydd's dad worked there for 30 years, initially unskilled, advancing to semi-skilled work as a welder and sand blaster. Dafydd to this day remains amazed that an Irishman and a monoglot Welsh speaker actually managed to understand each other in the first place.

George also had a girlfriend called Edie who had a friend called Gwendolyn. Gwendolyn was to become Dafydd's mother.

Dafydd's dad received his call-up papers for the war. He and Gwendolyn went off to Southend for him to enlist, but it was decreed that he was involved in essential manufacturing work for the war effort, so he remained at home, although, in addition to his day job, spent most nights on duty at a fire station with the Auxiliary Fire Service.

Dafydd was born in December 1944.

# 2

# First Generation Welsh

DAFYDD GREW UP feeling entirely Welsh.

One of the major influences on this was his father's inability to speak fluent English. Dafydd needed to focus from an early age on his father's English and how it was influenced by the Welsh language; for example, his father would frequently mistakenly place the adjective after the noun. There was also his north Wales accent to contend with. Over time Dafydd almost became his father's translator, as even in later years his father's English was only what Dafydd describes as the equivalent of our Level 2 or 3 with Welsh learners.

They spoke English in the house, but if working together in the garden his father would often speak to Dafydd in Welsh. And if his father received a letter from north Wales, he would read it at the table, put it down, and without realising it, begin speaking in Welsh. 'You're speaking Welsh,' Dafydd's mother would say. 'No I'm bloody well not,' came the reply. Dafydd's dad did however have some opportunity to speak the language with Welsh colleagues at work, and the Welsh newspaper, *Y Cymro*, was delivered weekly to the house.

Friends would explain to Dafydd that they couldn't understand his father, although at times he would purposely get things wrong. Then after they had said 'Pardon?' to him for the third time, his father would respond in jest, 'What's the matter, can't I speak bloody English?' Dafydd would reply, 'No, actually you can't'.

In the absence of any Welsh lessons in school, Dafydd worked hard at teaching himself the language, spending his half-a-crowns on such books as *Learn Welsh in a Week* and *Teach Yourself Welsh*. When studying for his O level in French he would also replicate his French grammar by undertaking the same exercises in Welsh.

When he had to sit his French oral exam, he answered the examiner's questions about holidays by mentioning his visits to the farm in north Wales. The examiner then asked in French whether Dafydd was actually Welsh. The examiner also turned out to be Welsh and a Welsh speaker. The conversation ended with them speaking to each other more in Welsh than in French, and the examiner's wink as Dafydd left the room was a clear indication that there wouldn't be a problem with him passing the examination.

Dafydd's father was obviously pleased that his son was attempting to learn Welsh, and gave him all the help he could, always shouting out the answers to Dafydd's questions, but he just couldn't explain the reasoning behind many of the linguistic points. His Welsh was of the vernacular. He had no understanding of the subtleties of Welsh grammar. Dafydd would ask about the rules of mutation, of why *cath* becomes *gath*. 'Because it bloody well does,' came the reply. Dafydd remains disappointed that his father was unable to explain more. Dafydd has always needed to know the reasoning behind grammatical points but he learnt over time it was sensible not to ask why. His father, like most Welshmen according to Dafydd, had a short fuse, although his rants were fairly innocuous and short-lived.

The other motivation for Dafydd to learn Welsh were the trips to the farm at Llithfaen. Each summer, the family would spend the annual 'factory fortnight' helping out on the farm, with his parents in later years leaving Dafydd there on his own for the rest of the summer school holidays.

Dafydd loved it. Working on the farm. Playing with the local kids. He would excitedly count the days to his summer holidays. And he would work hard at his Welsh prior to making the trip each year.

He was especially influenced by his relationship with his *Taid*. Although not his biological grandfather, there was a close relationship between the two, and *Taid* was very pleased and proud that Dafydd had chosen to call him by that name. On one occasion, the rest of the family went away to Scotland on holidays, leaving Dafydd and *Taid* to run the farm on their own. His aunt was amazed that they managed, given that Welsh was their only means of communication.

Dafydd adored his *Taid*. He saw him as a gentle man, a philosopher. On one occasion Dafydd recalls walking from the farmhouse across the fields when some rooks started eating the corn. Dafydd picked up a rock to throw at the birds. '*Paid*' (stop), said *Taid*, 'I've put enough in the ground for them as well'. He was well aware of the whole chain of nature. He knew everything that there was to know about the farm and its animals. He was his own vet, and was always devising ingenious schemes around the farm. He used to dose the cattle with medicine from elderberry wine dispensed from a cow horn. When some of the cows were suckling other cows for milk, he devised a muzzle to put round the mouths of the offending cows with nails attached to make sure they got a kick in the teeth if they ever again approached another cow. He was a national champion as both a sheepdog trialist and a dry-stone wall builder. But he never travelled outside Wales.

The family in Llithfaen made huge efforts to welcome both Dafydd and his father, the 'prodigal son', and not forgetting his mother, for whom the holidays were also great fun. And the highlight of every Christmas was a parcel from the farm with a big fattened cockerel, churned butter, and of course a long letter in Welsh for Dafydd's father.

Dafydd never came across any anti-English feeling, and while his grandparents and cousins were totally Welsh, and only spoke Welsh all day and every day, they were happy in their Welshness and had no reason to resent the English in the manner of us exiles. When Welsh extremists began burning holiday cottages, it occurred to Dafydd to ask his cousin Glyn whether he knew anyone involved. Glyn was as shocked to be asked as he was angry that such things were happening at all. There was in fact a caravan on the farm rented out to visitors, many of them of course English.

Dafydd did however encounter what I referred to in an earlier chapter as 'two-tier' pricing. In later years, while calling in the local shop on the way to the beach, the shopkeeper heard Dafydd speaking to his children in English, so did likewise, in handing him the bill. 'That's a lot of money,' Dafydd then said to her in Welsh. 'You're Welsh!' replied the shopkeeper, grabbing the bill back to recalculate the figure. It was Dafydd's turn to be shocked and angry.

Dafydd grew up with a strong sense of Welshness thanks to his father. And the local Essex environment in which he grew up didn't intrude sufficiently to counter this sense of identity. The village of East Hanningfield was fairly isolated with the local bus running every two hours, only to Chelmsford. The family didn't have television. They did listen to the radio, but his father was a sports fanatic and this meant supporting Wales in everything, especially football, rugby and boxing. Dafydd recalls his father once waking him up at two in the morning to listen on the radio to Dai Dower, Welsh, British and Empire flyweight champion, fighting somewhere overseas.

The local bobby was also Welsh and a Welsh speaker, but from Swansea, so while he and Dafydd's father always conversed in Welsh, they would often laugh at how they didn't entirely understand each other. The policeman spoke English to Dafydd.

Dafydd's mother was from a large local family. Her father was a bricklayer, but spent most of his time and money down the pub. She wasn't sporting, so didn't become involved in Dafydd's and his father's support for Wales, and she liked to hear the two of them talking in Welsh. She must have been aware of, and sympathetic to, her husband's language needs. They were very close as a couple.

It was from his mum and not his dad however that Dafydd developed a Welshman's love of music. She and Dafydd both loved hymn singing and male voice choirs. And she would play him classical records on their wind-up gramophone from an early age. Dafydd's father, on the other hand, described himself as the only Welshman who couldn't sing; although he still liked to listen.

Dafydd used to sing in the church choir, perform as a bell ringer, and also attend Sunday school in a mission hut in the village run by Salvationists, where the teacher, Mrs Ford, offered Dafydd music lessons for free if he would play the harmonium at the church services. Later, as a student, he would go round the pubs playing his guitar, and sing in the choirs of the various schools in which he was to teach.

In Llithfaen, he used to attend local chapels just for the hymn singing, sometimes accompanying his aunt who has been an organist in one of the chapels for over 50 years, and is still playing in her eighties. Dafydd would, in later years, go in search of the folk music, as well as hymns, known to be sung in various north Wales pubs. Like myself he can phonetically sing a dozen Welsh hymns without really understanding the words he is singing.

Dafydd knew he was Welsh from his father and from Llithfaen. But he didn't make waves to mix with Welsh people in the London area. His Welshness as a child was mostly of the mind, a private affair. He doesn't think of himself as a Welshman in exile, but merely as a Welshman. He doesn't possess any of the sense of deprivation that exiles like myself carry as baggage. He only reacts negatively if he gets called English, and remains disappointed at the missed opportunity to learn more Welsh from his father.

# 3

# Welsh On Hold

BEING WELSH, DAFYDD wanted from an early age to be, not an engine driver or a fireman, but a teacher.

He went to a brand new, modern comprehensive school in the Essex village of Sandon, followed by sixth-form at the more traditional, all boys, King George VI Grammar School in Chelmsford. He loved the comprehensive school, 'a breath of fresh air', with a modern headmaster who forbade corporal punishment. He also felt he was taught really well there. He was known as 'Taffy', but, being a big, quite strong lad, was never bullied.

He trained as a teacher at Borough Road College in Isleworth, then, at the same time as his first teaching post, studied part-time for a further four years, for a maths degree at the then Kingston Polytechnic. Given his time over again, the degree would have come first.

During his three years at Borough Road he was a permanent member of the football first XI. He didn't initially intend to play, but, watching the early season trials in his first year, he thought he was a match for those on the field, so raced home on the very first weekend, much to the surprise of his parents, to pick up his boots. He missed the trials but made the first XI by the third week.

His first teaching posts were in secondary modern and comprehensive schools in Feltham in south-west London, followed by four years at a South Wimbledon High School. Since 1975 he has taught at Brooklands College of Further Education in Weybridge, Surrey, becoming head in turn of the maths and computing departments. He then started an

IT department, introducing computers to the whole of the college. In retirement, he still lectures in maths one day a week to undergraduate engineers.

During his early time as a probationary teacher he met his wife-to-be, Sandy, on a blind date at Twickenham station. They were married in 1969. Sandy was born in India, daughter of an army father. She went to boarding school in India, even speaking Hindu.

She enjoyed his Welshness, tolerating his support for Welsh teams and his love of *Songs of Praise* (if it featured a Welsh chapel) on Sunday night television. But for the next 25 years Dafydd seldom visited Llithfaen, except for the occasional funeral. For holidays he instead took his children camping, in search of the sun. North Wales would have meant working on the farm.

Sandy and Dafydd divorced in the year 2000. Dafydd's new partner, Mary, is first generation Irish. Her mother spoke a smattering of Gaelic as a child, and envies Dafydd going to Welsh classes. And Mary is now happy to test Dafydd on his Welsh verbs and vocabulary. But Mary really sees herself as English.

Both Sandy and Mary are essentially city girls, so retiring to a Welsh rural retreat was always unlikely, although Dafydd did many years ago suddenly have the urge to forsake the city and take up sheep farming in Wales. The urge blew over.

Sandy and Dafydd had two daughters. Thanks to Dafydd, both girls knew the odd Welsh word and could count to ten in Welsh by the time they were five. But neither claim to be Welsh. Kathryn studied medicine in Cardiff 'not because she is Welsh but because she liked the sound of the course'. For whatever reason, she has fallen in love with Wales, and now lectures in Cardiff, while at the same time working part-time as a GP in Brynmawr. She and Dafydd visited the National Eisteddfod when it was held in Ebbw Vale last year, only to be confronted by patient after patient of Kathy's when crossing the *maes*.

Susie is an anaesthetist working in Torquay. She has no obvious interest in Welshness, but she can still count to ten in Welsh.

Dafydd's mam and dad passed away within six months of each other in the mid 1990s. His dad, in his eighties, was hospitalised after a fall and died of pneumonia. Strangely, for the last four weeks of his life, he lost all recall of the English language, so the hospital stationed a Welsh-speaking nurse on the ward to care for him. Coming from south Wales, communication was still a struggle.

# 4

# Eisteddfodau, London Welsh Centre and Nant Gwrtheyrn

DAFYDD HAS MAINTAINED an emotional contact with Wales over time.

He is not religious, but he loves the atmosphere of chapels and the singing of Welsh hymns, and visits the National Eisteddfod most years to experience the *cymanfa ganu* (singing festival) and *côr meibion* (male choir) competitions.

For the recent Bala Eisteddfod, Dafydd stayed in a small hotel in the town itself. While eating on his own in the restaurant, he eavesdropped on the conversation at the next table in an attempt to improve his Welsh. He was spotted and invited to join the table, which turned out to be occupied by Bryn Terfel's mum and dad. Prior to knowing their identity he had foolishly inquired as to whether they or any of their family had actually performed at the Eisteddfod.

Dafydd and Mary have also been welcomed to Llithfaen on several occasions, and last year all the cousins and their offspring got together for a long weekend in Cardiff. Cousin Alwyn now runs the farm, cousin Gwyn is a Baptist minister in Bala running a youth centre, and a third cousin, Glyn, teaches maths and IT through the medium of Welsh. He is one of only a handful of A level examiners in the subject across the whole of Wales.

In retirement, Dafydd has decided to try harder to improve his Welsh, as otherwise 'I'm going to be on my deathbed not speaking the language of my fathers!'

Despite the early summers at Llithfaen, and conversations with his father, his ability to speak the language has deteriorated over the years since leaving home. He has always dabbled with learning the language, but only now has made the time to study it more seriously, with the goal of achieving greater literacy, to read as well as speak it.

Three years ago he enrolled for classes at the London Welsh Centre, and has also tried City Lit for a year. He doesn't want to sit examinations, just read and speak the language, and mix with Welsh people. Evenings at Gray's Inn Road have become one of the highlights of his week, and he regrets not seeking out Welsh people in London earlier in his life.

His daughters also, as a combined Christmas and birthday present, bought him a week's course at Nant Gwrtheryn, the only permanent residential college teaching Welsh to adults in the whole of Wales. It just happens to be adjacent to the village of Llithfaen, a mere couple of miles from his cousin's farm, Llithfaen Isaf.

Nant Gwrtheryn is described on the website 'The Attractions in Snowdonia' as 'a magical place, a remote Victorian quarry village set on a 200 acre site in a secluded wooded valley overlooking Porthdinllaen Bay... where you are free to wander under the watchful gaze of choughs (crows), peregrine falcons and wild goats, and sometimes in the company of seals and dolphins'.

Welsh has been taught at 'The Nant' since 1982, when the Nant Gwrtheryn Trust, a registered charity, was formed through the efforts of Dr Carl Clowes, a local GP, and others, who bought the village and set about renovating the old buildings after its days as a hippie commune. Since then more than 25,000 people have learnt Welsh at the centre, and a complete £5m renovation was opened by First Minister Carwyn Jones in 2009, with four-star accommodation now being provided for up to 80 residential guests.

The Nant also functions as a Heritage Centre, bringing much needed employment to the area, and receiving more than 30,000 day visitors a year. The earliest archaeological evidence of inhabitation in the area are the two Iron Age hill forts which dominate the high ground above the valley. But the main focus of the new heritage displays, in the old chapel and a 'period house', offer an insight into life in the granite quarry village which existed from 1870 up to the First World War, then later for a brief period in the early 1930s. Around 1910, there were three quarries employing and barracking 2,000 men to produce road stone setts, which were then exported by sea to build the cobbled streets of Manchester and Liverpool.

Dafydd's father had worked in one of the quarries, Carreg y Llam, and wandering along the Heritage Path in a break from Welsh lessons, Dafydd came across a photograph of quarry workers from about 1930. There in the centre of the photograph he spotted his father.

It was as if Dafydd and his father had returned home together.

The next chapter looks at two further first generation exiles, one of Welsh descent born in London, the other of English descent born in Colwyn Bay, for whom the local environment in which they were brought up was to have more of a significant influence on their chosen Welsh identity.

# First Generation

**David Daniel**

**Tony Fielden**

David Daniel, Dai to his fellow Welsh learners at the London Welsh Centre *(Canolfan Cymry Llundain)* in Gray's Inn Road, was born in Paddington of Welsh parents.

Dai is very much a Londoner, but grew up in a chapel-based London Welsh community and maintained strong links with his parents' family in Alan Rees's Glanaman. He has, as a result, very much taken on a Welsh identity, become pretty conversant in the Welsh language, albeit with a broad north London accent, made himself extremely knowledgeable about Welsh history and politics, and become heavily involved in the London Welsh Centre, sitting on the entertainments committee and editing the centre's quarterly magazine.

Conversely, Tony Fielden, a fellow resident in Radlett, Hertfordshire, was born in Colwyn Bay, north Wales, of English parents.

I first came across Tony Fielden at Radlett's Men's Club extolling the virtues of the Welsh rugby team in the face of ribald comments from most of the other members. He clearly identifies with his childhood community in Colwyn Bay, and even his English Chester-born son is equally vociferous in support of all things Welsh.

Both Dai and Tony, despite their different backgrounds, feel more Welsh than English, and hold as dear those values that I have begun to identify as being at the core of Welshness.

# David Daniel

1

# Glanaman Origins

DAI DANIEL'S FAMILY hailed from Glanaman, but in his search for work, Dai's grandfather had emigrated to Canada, mainly working on the railways. Even in Canada, the family still maintained its Welshness, with Welsh being the language of the home, and the family being very involved in the chapel and music, *cymanfaoedd canu* and eisteddfodau. They returned to Glanaman when Dai's father was in his late teens.

It was here that he met Dai's mum. And mirroring the divisions so typical of the area – also the home of Alan Rees – his father Tegryd had become a metalworker and staunch Labour, while mother Nansi was of farming stock, and therefore nonconformist and Liberal. She would, later in life, vote Tory on specific issues despite being a good friend of long-standing Llanelli Labour MP, Jim Griffiths, and having a first cousin, Airwyn Morgan, professor of theology at Bangor, who became one of Plaid Cymru's first parliamentary candidates in the 1950s.

Dai's mum had wanted to get married before his father went off to war, but Tegryd didn't want to leave her a young widow, or come back to her 'in bits'. He didn't think it would be fair on her.

But they got engaged: on the station platform, as she came to see him off to the war. It was another six years before they saw each other again.

Nansi was grammar school educated, and due to go, where else, but to Aber (University College of Wales, Aberystwyth). This was put on hold as she went to work for the Air Ministry, firstly in Stroud, then in London, ending up in the Foreign Office. She did quite well, spent time in the consulate in Madrid, and there was the possibility in 1948 of being posted to India, although with the religious unrest at the time, it was decided that this would not be a safe place for a woman.

After Dai was born, Nansi worked part-time for a Jewish property company, Bloomfield, owners of the Kensington Garden Hotel.

Home from the war, Dai's dad found work, as part of a large Welsh contingent, in the heavily unionised car plant in Cowley, Oxford. Nansi was at the time living in digs with a Welsh family, typically running a dairy in Notting Hill. Tegryd would come down to London from Oxford at weekends, and help with the milk round, delivering to, among others, mass murderer Reg Christie, even chatting to him as he delivered the milk. Christie was hanged in 1953 after being found guilty of strangling at least six women at 10 Rillington Place, Notting Hill. A tenant of Christie's, Timothy Evans, was originally found guilty of two of the murders, his own wife and daughter, and wrongly hanged for the crimes in 1950. The falsely-accused Timothy Evans was also a visitor to the shop, Dai's mum recalling him as 'a bit of a daydreamer'.

There was still a huge family back in Glanaman. Dai's grandparents came from large families, so there was plenty of opportunity for Dai to spend all of his school holidays down in Glanaman.

Dai doesn't think he has met a Daniel from that part of Wales to whom he is not related, and he recently had the opportunity to put his theory to the test. On meeting another David Daniel in Welsh Learners, they talked and compared notes, and Dai found his mum knew the family, relatives of his father's people. As Dai puts it, 'another Daniel had failed to escape'.

## 2

# We Are What We Are

As a young child Dai never thought much about his nationality. His parents were well travelled, certainly compared to the family back in Glanaman, and being brought up in London he was aware that many of his friends spoke different languages at home, ate different foods and held different religious beliefs, without these differences affecting their friendship.

And he was made aware of what else was open to you. His father wouldn't deprive him of anything. Tegryd detested football – 'sissies kissing each other after scoring a goal' – but in London you take your son to football, so he would take Dai with his mates to see Chelsea or QPR, Fulham or Arsenal. (There were also visits to London Welsh at Old Deer Park several times a season.)

London is very much a global village, big and diverse, so where you were brought up becomes irrelevant. Dai has an affection for London, but not to any specific area, including Cheshunt where he now lives. I detect a similar ambivalence in my daughter, who has no affection for where she was brought up in Bushey, Hertfordshire.

Having said that, Dai 'wouldn't be seen dead south of the river!' What is it about the Thames that divides people so?

But Dai did acquire a Welsh identity, as a result of home, the chapel and the larger family back in Wales. He simply knew he was a Welsh boy in London.

English became Dai's first language because it was the language of school, of the playground, and the common denominator among all his friends from their different ethnic and cultural backgrounds. But at home he was brought up listening to both English and Welsh languages. His mum and dad spoke English when in company but spoke Welsh to each other. They were both fluent in Welsh, but his mother spoke Welsh to him and his father spoke English to ensure he became conversant with both languages.

Tegryd belonged to the Hammersmith Welsh Male Voice Choir, and on Friday nights the house would be full of Welsh lads meeting up before choir practice. There would also always be relatives from Glanaman staying in the house.

The local dairy was, typically, Welsh-owned by friends of the family back in Glanaman, and the barber in Shirland Road was a deacon of its Welsh chapel, later to be merged with Willesden Green chapel.

It was the chapel which kept the Welsh community together. On Sundays Willesden Green chapel was always bursting at the seams. Everyone was made extremely welcome, and Dai, along with 30 other kids of Welsh-speaking parents, attended Sunday school, from 12 noon right through to the six o'clock evening service: six hours in a very Welsh environment.

They were taught to read and write in Welsh, received scripture lessons in Welsh, performed nativity plays in Welsh, and gave *adroddiadau* (recitations) to the packed chapel at Sunday morning service. They even performed at eisteddfod *y plant* (children's eisteddfod) held annually in Red Lion Square.

Whether you spoke Welsh or not, you understood what was going on. No one gave it a second thought. Most of the kids could hold their own in Welsh, although only a few were really fluent in the language.

They also had time to play together, kicking a football in the vestry or in between the gravestones. And there was a snooker table and table tennis in the Welsh school which shared the chapel premises. As they grew older many of them used to play table tennis there on Friday nights. Dai most probably saw me losing my two finals in the Welsh Chapels Table Tennis Championships at the very same venue.

The kids hailed from all parts of north London, and after Sunday school went off to their different schools on Monday mornings to meet up again as friends a week later. Dai and six others all got confirmed at 15, and away from the chapel, at school in Marylebone, and where he lived in Kingsbury, Dai became 'the token Taff'.

One cannot underestimate the contribution of the network of London Welsh chapels to the preservation of Welshness, and in particular the Welsh language, among first generation exiles.

Sadly, the chapel in Willesden is no longer, although the Welsh school still survives in nearby Stonebridge Park.

Wilbur, from the bowls club, and his wife Liz, like Dai's parents, are also both fluent Welsh speakers, Wilbur hailing from Llanelli's Seaside, Liz from Machynlleth in mid Wales. Living in Staines, south-west of London, they did not however have the advantage of a local Welsh chapel around which a Welsh-speaking community could have developed. Their three children grew up initially speaking Welsh at home, but eventually fell out of the habit. Wilbur felt that to give pre-eminence at home to Welsh would only see the children suffer in their school work conducted, obviously, in English.

A further complication was the fact that two of the three offspring were twins who, when young, created a language of their own. Three languages were a bit too much to handle.

Wilbur's family have since become a veritable United Nations, with his daughters marrying an Australian and a Yorkshireman, and his son marrying a Slovakian. Wilbur is clearly doing his bit for international cooperation and unity.

Dai on the other hand was still bound to his family in Wales. As well as being part of the Welsh chapel community, once the school term ended Dai was packed off to Glanaman three or four times a year and usually for the whole of the summer.

Glanaman became another home. As he was prepared to make some effort to converse in Welsh, he became quickly accepted by his cousins' friends, who also visited him in London.

He was immediately recognised locally in Glanaman: 'Aren't you Nansi and Tegryd's little boy?' They would all cross his palm with silver, as was the custom in those days, even though he didn't have a clue who many of them were.

He became part of the family, and a big family it was. On one occasion he got lost from his cousins at the top of a disused pit. Fortunately, the driver of a passing car who came to his rescue turned out to be his mother's first cousin. And in later beer drinking years he would always be in his cousins' corner in their fights (literally) with neighbouring Brynaman boys.

Despite being a Londoner through and through and never having lived in Wales, Dai confesses to a sense of *hiraeth*, a longing for home, on crossing the Severn Bridge. He is wary of confessing to this for fear of being laughed out of court, and he can't make any sense of it. But he still feels this strong deep down affinity with Glanaman and Wales in general.

# 3

# The Awakening of an Identity

DAI WAS AND is an avid reader, particularly of history books. His father wasn't well educated, but, in true Welsh style, he encouraged his son in his reading, Dai eventually going on to study for a degree in politics at Hull University.

In his early teens, Dai would pick up the *Western Mail* for the rugby results from Griff's, a Welsh bookshop in Leicester Square, whose coffee shop was a favourite meeting place of London chapel Welsh.

It was here that he came across *Wales and the Welsh* by Trevor Fishlock. The author was of Welsh descent, the book being written on his return to Wales in 1972 after many years abroad as staff correspondent of *The Times* in India and New York, and Moscow bureau chief for *The Daily Telegraph*. Later, in 2008, he was named a judge for the Wales Book of the Year Award.

Dai describes as a further seminal moment the reading of *The Welsh Extremist* written by Ned Thomas in the aftermath of the protests over the investiture of Charles as Prince of Wales in 1969.

Ned Thomas was also able to bring a broad perspective to his writings from time spent as a journalist and teacher in both Spain and the Soviet Union. Then from 1970 to 1990 he lectured in English at Aberystwyth, and edited the magazine *Planet*. From 1990 to 1998 he was director of the University of Wales Press, and more recently became the director of the Mercator Project on Minority Language Media in the European Union. He chaired the company set up to publish the first ever daily paper in Welsh, *Y Byd*, which unfortunately never came to fruition, and is also currently a board member of Academi, recently relaunched as Literature Wales, the Welsh national literature promotion agency and society for authors.

These books, therefore, weren't writings by bigoted, narrow-minded souls who had never left Wales, but the thoughts of talented and well-informed travellers.

Ned Thomas quotes Emrys ap Iwan, claiming that, even in the 19th century, spending some time abroad, or with a foreign literature, was a way of making a Welshman more conscious of his own Welsh identity. It helped him separate out what in his own background was distinct from the English culture. Education and travel do not make the Welshman less concerned with his own tradition but more aware of it. On returning to Wales from France, Emrys ap Iwan was able to stand apart from the provincial movement of 'getting on' through English among the rising Welsh middle class, and to appreciate that they were losing much more than they were gaining.

These books represented Dai's first exposure to Welsh history. He had always felt it a grave injustice that it did not form any part of the history lessons which he received in school. His history teacher even borrowed one of his books to learn something about Welsh history. Such books gave voice to Dai's feelings, articulating them, not in the manner of political pamphlets, but as writings of quality, persuasively spoken from the heart.

Dai's perceptions of his Welsh identity, plus the recognition of the major efforts people have made to preserve such an identity, crucially stem from reading these books and others.

Trevor Fishlock observed that, 'Most Welshmen love Wales more than most Englishmen love England'. He talks of Welshmen in conversation jokingly challenging each other to see if they can go for at least 10 minutes without mentioning Wales.

This love of Wales and Welshness is probably on two counts. Firstly, the Welsh enjoy sharing their basic love of humanity, of community, even of argument: 'Wales is nine-tenths a conquered country, and the unconquered bit is not territory but the character of the people and the qualities of the Welsh way of life.'

Secondly, being dominated by their much larger neighbour has necessitated focusing on their history and culture to ensure it doesn't disappear entirely: 'Englishmen take for granted the prestige of their country and their ubiquitous language and the security of admired values and the way of life. Welshmen do not have that luxury.'

Ned Thomas picks up on the same argument: 'The Englishman is remarkably unself-conscious about his language. The Welsh speaker self-consciously buys Welsh books, starts Welsh school. The Welsh speaker has to assert his identity, because this identity will otherwise not be respected.'

The loss of an independent Welsh identity from England was initially formalised in the Laws of Wales Act of 1536, and a more detailed Act of 1542. The ascent of a Welshman, Henry Tudor, to the throne in 1485 had proved to be a pyrrhic victory, and while these Acts of Union gave Welshmen the same rights as Englishmen, the English language held sway in English courts and Welsh noblemen could only benefit if they both spoke English and moved to London.

English became the language of government and business; Welsh became the language of the scullery and the farmyard. A further consequence was that the preservation of Welsh culture was left in the hands of the peasantry, *y gwerin*. Welsh culture became very much a culture of the people, who took up nonconformity in religion, and created far more of a democracy in their local politics.

A crucial lifeline to the preservation of the language, and therefore the culture, was ironically a 1588 Act of Parliament which decreed that the Bible should be translated into Welsh, with the specific objective of preserving the Protestant faith in Wales.

But in general terms, while freedom of speech has always

been claimed as a major tenet of English society and civilisation, this seems only to have been the case if that speech was in English.

A commission set up in 1847 to look at the state of education in Wales, known infamously and derisively as 'The Treason of the Blue Books', claimed that the Welsh language was a millstone round the neck of any ambitious Welshman, and it became a custom in schools to place a wooden collar, the Welsh Not, around the neck of any pupil heard to utter any words in Welsh. The collar would then be passed from pupil to pupil through the day whenever anyone was observed speaking Welsh. The last child to wear the collar was punished. Dai's Nan was caned several times for speaking Welsh in the schoolyard in Aberdare.

Also, over time, pupils in Welsh schools have learnt little of their country's history. The history taught is English history.

Ned Thomas quotes Anglo-Welsh writer, Glyn Jones, who speaks of his time in Merthyr Grammar School: 'The establishment might have been in the middle of The Broads, or up in the Pennines, for all the contact it had with the rich life of the community surrounding it. We had no school eisteddfod, we heard nothing of the turbulent industrial history of the town itself, nothing of its Welsh literary associations, nothing of its religious history.'

But the main crime of the English was not so much the enforcement of a language policy, but a dismissiveness which generated an inferiority in Welsh speakers. A 1682 pamphlet joked: 'Their native gibberish is usually prattled through the whole of Taphydom, except in their market towns whose inhabitants being a little raised do begin to despise it.'

Even an advanced educationist such as Matthew Arnold remarked as late as 1852 that: 'It must always be the desire of government to render its dominions... homogeneous. Sooner or later the differences of language between England and Wales will probably be effaced... an event which is socially and politically so desirable.'

And the picture is no different today. Friends in my own village, on learning of my efforts to relearn Welsh, ask 'Why on earth bother?' And a young assistant in the local florist, on seeing the Welsh message I had penned on a greetings card, was quite unaware that the language even existed. I am these days able, however, to log on at the doctor's surgery in Welsh!

Ned Thomas speaks of Welsh interests being wholly marginalised, not with malice or conspiracy but through being a bureaucratic nuisance. Carmarthen town, with its English law courts, was further away psychologically than it was geographically from the rural Carmarthenshire of Alan Rees and Dai Daniel's forbearers.

In business and commerce Wales was peripheral, with an inadequate road system in which the few major routes pointed east towards England. Southern Welshmen were, as a result, ostracised from their compatriots in the north. The M4 (plus the minute M48) is still the only motorway in Wales.

Parts of Wales will never be accessible to large markets, but where you build your roads and railways can be questions of a political and not just a commercial nature.

The coming of industrialisation was a two-edged sword. There was a vast amount of, largely English, immigration, but the Industrial Revolution also provided work for thousands of Welshmen who would otherwise have emigrated. And in the early part of the 20th century, Welsh speakers were still to be found in abundance among the industrial working class. But here again English was the language of formal business, and even trade union officials like Alan Rees's father, while speaking in Welsh in their everyday lives, spoke English when conducting official trade union business.

Trevor Fishlock observes that emigration continues to be a facet of the Welsh scene, with many educated youngsters leaving in search of employment, to be replaced by holidaymakers, the elderly from the Midlands and Merseyside, or immigrants from all parts of the UK without any identification with the local community.

Ned Thomas in 1971 describes Wales, in the context of the UK, as being 'a holiday playground, a source of energy, an artillery range'.

In 1850, two-thirds of the population spoke Welsh. This had declined to 50 per cent by 1900, and to 19 per cent by 1991.

Even those retaining their language were faced with their own peculiar difficulties. Ned Thomas remarks that:

> ... even among those who are from Welsh-speaking homes, few are educated in their own language and literature... Then there is the slovenliness of much spoken Welsh, the use of English borrowings when perfectly good Welsh words exist, the uncertainty about grammatical points, inevitable when little education has been given in the language, and when Welsh speakers are fed on English by the mass media... [and finally] to bring up one's children to speak the language requires a positive act.

Several human stories emerge of their predicament. Trevor Fishlock speaks of distinguished Welsh writers whose non-Welsh-speaking children are unable to read their works. Ned Thomas describes a novel by Kate Roberts about a family on the Llŷn Peninsula, in which the monoglot Welsh-speaking mother refuses to attend her son's graduation because she won't be able to understand the ceremony in English. She later receives a telegram informing her of another son's death in the First World War which she has to take to the local post office to have translated to learn the news.

Trevor Fishlock observes that it is difficult to write in Welsh about a society that doesn't speak it. And Ned Thomas points out that some Welsh speakers ended up writing in English because it was the language of their education. It also happens to be more profitable commercially.

Unfortunately such writings often feature stereotypical, rich fruity Welsh characterisation. Synthetic identity always arises from 'cultural imperialism', emphasising ersatz emblems such as the tartan and haggis for Scotland, and assuming Spain to be all castanets.

The British Council spreads the work of quite minor contemporary English writers around the world, and when a Welsh book is translated into English, it has as much chance of being bought by the Council as any other book. But a small language needs more. It needs such translations to be commissioned. The Council's investment is promoting English, not British, literature overseas. There is no pressure on the freedom of speech of Welsh writers, but there is a distinct lack of economic support.

Ned Thomas expounds: 'Who is better served? Small nations in the Soviet Union such as Georgia, whose writers are translated not only into Russian, but also into English and French, but always subject to ideological controls, or the Welsh, who have complete freedom to write what they like, but no economic power to make their literature known, while their money, like everyone else's in Britain, goes to boost English cultural prestige round the world?'

Problems were not only limited to the promotion of the written word. When Trevor Fishlock was writing in 1972 Wales – 'the land of culture' – had no national theatre, no national orchestra, no concert hall, no opera house.

Sir Geraint Evans, world-renowned tenor, threatened in 1971 never to sing again in Wales unless facilities for opera were improved: 'It is second best all the time... and I'm fed up with seeing second best in Wales.' Welsh culture equated to community art developed without patronage, a nation of 'amateur singers'.

Turning to the media, Ned Thomas suggests that the UK is 'a state where press and television are the most centralised in the world'. Daily newspapers are London-based, often with no regional editions. These papers feature little news from Wales, which not only gives Welsh people little sense of identity, but also fails to inform the English public of the sense of frustration felt by the Welsh. This only serves to engender an attitude of dismissiveness on the part of our English neighbours which further exacerbates the situation.

The protests of the Welsh Language Society in the late 1960s only received attention from the English press when they were seen as a threat to Prince Charles's investiture in 1969.

The so-called national press, based in London, had, and have no Welsh editions. Television and radio were 'an imposed system', initially with no specific Welsh regional offering, with north and south Wales independently amalgamated with their adjacent English regions.

The introduction of Welsh-language programming in the 1960s only amounted to a minimal number of off-peak hours. These were transmitted on the main channels, rather than as an independent offering, so to receive them Welsh viewers had to forego simultaneously transmitted English-language programmes. This only served to annoy non-Welsh-speaking Welshmen and exacerbated the widening divide between them and Welsh speakers.

As the proportion of Welsh speakers has reduced through the course of the 20th century, so Wales has almost become a divided country, with the demands of Welsh speakers being countered by monoglot English speakers who resent the intrusion of the Welsh language into their lives. And the debates about the perpetuation of a national identity are as much internal as pointing the finger at our English neighbours.

Trevor Fishlock speaks of a Welshman who announced that he would prefer to come back to earth as an Englishman so that he could avoid all this self-analysis and self-justifying defensive attitude. But Ned Thomas argues that the English-speaking and Welsh-speaking Welsh are not two quite separate language groups like the English and French speakers in Quebec Province, Canada. They are one group, one family, one nation, which has suffered a split in its consciousness, and this produces a curious emotional ambivalence.

The Welsh-language community is a series of overlapping groups, and some of these overlap with the non-Welsh-speaking

Welsh. And there is a fluidity about these linguistic boundaries, with older Welshmen often merely hanging on to a residual knowledge of Welsh, yet younger English-speaking Welshmen driven to teach themselves Welsh.

Ned Thomas in 1971 speaks of still meeting 'Welsh people of the older generation who think it is in some way better to speak English. We have been both secretly proud of, and publicly apologetic for, our language... These older Welsh speakers have a deference to the English language inseparable for centuries from deference to the higher social class.'

Then there were (less now I hope) monoglot English-speaking Welshmen who strongly objected to the intrusion of the Welsh language into their daily lives:

'If everyone speaks English, what's the point (of speaking Welsh); they'd be better off teaching them French and German.'

'Something got up by a few hooligans and intellectuals in north Wales and kept going by stupid newspapermen. It really makes my blood boil.'

'It's these nationalists. They make me sick with their demands for more Welsh. Why do my kids have to sit through Welsh lessons just because these fanatics hold the reins?'

According to Ned Thomas, 'the English speaker is held down more than the Welsh speaker. The crisis confers a dignity on the Welsh speaker once he abandons his passive acceptance of inferiority. But the English-speaking Welshman can easily feel unaccepted either into the Welsh/Welsh or English/English community.'

On the other hand, there is an ever-increasing number of English-speaking Welshmen hungry to learn Welsh and establish contact with their heritage and culture. And Welsh speakers must realise that any future for the Welsh language must depend largely on these English speakers in Wales.

Trevor Fishlock observed that there was a large body of parents who had only goodwill for Welsh, and wanted their children to learn it, although they did not have the language themselves. English-speaking parents having a Welsh-speaking child has a developing cachet in smart middle class neighbourhoods, a certain trendiness in English-speaking circles.

Various friends and colleagues of Trevor were of like mind:

'My parents spoke Welsh but they never wanted me to learn it. They thought it was a bit second rate. But I'm earning my living in Wales, and moving a lot in circles where Welsh is widely used. It makes me wish I could speak it... I feel I'm missing something.'

'I'm a Welshman and it just seemed so ridiculous that I could not speak my native language... If you ask what the motive was I suppose that the truth is that I felt humiliated that I did not possess my native language.'

And from David John Underhill, a lorry driver from Bridgend, acquitted in the Free Wales Army trial of 1969:

It is difficult for you who are born Welsh speakers to understand how much the language can mean to us who are born without it. The Bridgend area has lost its Welsh entirely. The first time I came into contact with the language was at the National Eisteddfod in Aberafan. I asked someone to translate a Welsh sentence. It read, "A nation without language is a nation without heart" (*Cenedl heb iaith; cenedl heb galon*), and it was these words that started my interest in the language. I came to know about the Act of Union and the "Welsh Not" policy in the schools. This was why the language had died out in Bridgend. I promised myself I would learn the language and I joined an evening class. By today I can speak Welsh fairly fluently.

It is also easy to forget that both Dafydd Williams, one time secretary of Plaid Cymru, and Gwynfor Evans, long-time president of Plaid, were both English speakers by upbringing.

The remaining group in the population are the first-language Welsh speakers themselves, who as a minority have had to make strenuous efforts to preserve their language and culture.

The contention of both authors is that there is absolutely no credence to the argument that the efforts to promote the Welsh language are misplaced because they work on behalf of a mere 20 per cent minority. Such promotion is totally acceptable purely as a matter of democracy. Every minority has an unquestioned right to preserve its language and culture.

Professor T J Morgan of Swansea University once argued: 'How can we who are conditioned in favour of a bilingual policy win over the passive and innocently unconvinced?... The urge to survive does not depend upon arguments and evidence for its justification: the desire is its own justification. The concept of survival can be applied to the language, for in the make-up of many of us the language is an extension of ourselves.'

Trevor Fishlock adds that it is 'quite irrelevant to say Welsh speakers can speak English anyway. It's unrealistic to expect culturally aware people to stand by, inactive, while the soul of their nationality and community slips into quicksand.'

The fight to preserve the language is fundamental to the preservation of the totality of the Welsh culture. In Ned Thomas's words: 'By its existence, the language tells us that we are Welsh. All the feelings of nationality that are supported for Englishmen by the Queen, the Houses of Parliament, London policemen, bewigged judges, and a whole range of political, cultural and popular institutions rests for the Welshman on the language and literature.'

In 1968 Mrs Eirene White, a Minister of State at the Welsh Office, stated that 'It is the thoughts to be clothed that matter. Language is but the style in which it is dressed'. Ned Thomas counters that it is far more than that. 'Languages are very delicate networks of historically accumulated associations.' How do you translate the words *hiraeth* or *hwyl*, for example, into English? Trevor Fishlock aptly describes language as 'an identity disc'.

A further strand to the argument is that the existence of

a range of different individual cultures provides variety and humanity, a counter-culture, in the face of the 'crushing uniformity' of current life.

'Britain will be a poorer place if it cannot afford a little room and tolerance for the language which has answered for this civilised corner for more than fifteen centuries. It's part of a larger pattern. The modern emphasis is on economic growth, centralisation, large corporations and bureaucracies, and the inclination to examine human endeavour in terms of profit and usefulness, which tends to push individual and community needs and feelings into the background. Respect for people and their dignity has been lessened.' (Trevor Fishlock)

The move to a more open Europe has helped the cause, with small regions gaining greater recognition at the expense of the larger nations. 'Modern cultures are local and international, not national and provincial.' (Ned Thomas)

We must also squash the belief that preserving an ancient heritage is necessarily backward rather than forward looking. People can gain experience, strength, even solace from the past to help them face the future. You only have to look at Catalonia, eastern Europe, even Israel.

'In a country where so few outward things tell you that you are Welsh, [remembering] adds a quality of depth to the consciousness, a pole of resistance to the constant suggestion that we should forget and be content and, above all, consume. Even the landscape takes on a different quality if you are one of those who remember.' (Ned Thomas)

'People will not look forward to posterity, who never look backward to their ancestors.' (arch conservative, Edmund Burke)

'Tradition should be like a skeleton, inside the body, giving strength, not outside, like a hard shell of a crab, holding the life in.' (Unamuno, a Basque separatist)

Having argued the case for preserving and maintaining the independence of Wales's language and culture, the final question addressed by both Fishlock and Thomas is whether the end justifies the means. How extreme should our protest be?

Trevor Fishlock observed that the Welsh have a strong pacifist streak: 'Others turn to fists and guns, Welshmen form committees; courteous, easy-going and given to procrastination; a strong community spirit allied to their absorbing interest in things of the mind.'

I remember personally being strangely ambivalent on hearing about the deaths of Welsh extremists blowing themselves up before the investiture of 1969: a sense of self-righteousness in support of Welshmen who needed to be heard, mixed with a sense of guilt that my countrymen could possibly be using violent means against a democratic authority whom I had been brought up to respect.

But Ned Thomas argues very cogently that:

> If Britain cannot guarantee people the right to exist within their own culture, then it cannot expect these people to be over-scrupulous towards its own democratic institutions… We are asked to be tolerant of the status quo which is not tolerant of our language.
>
> Social change as well as Welsh change is limited by the system. Marginal innovation is claimed as exciting. Pressure from the centre, the government committee sits, the pressure group gives evidence, PR firms put the best case, and there is a small compromise to change.
>
> Discussing Welsh nationalism with Englishmen I get caught up in a kind of sixth-form debate about constitutions and boundaries. But they are not the starting point, not the source of deepest feelings. Young people are not dying for Wales because of a vision of a Welsh parliament in Cardiff, or the emblems of nationhood, but because they see a language and a culture and an identity being wiped off the map of the world, and no longer believe that the forms of British democracy can be used to prevent this.

On returning to Wales, Ned Thomas saw, not the ritual

sparring of the British political parties, but total politics as he had observed it, having lived in Spain and the Soviet Union, politics in which the control of institutions was all important:

> The Welsh pattern is one in which militancy certainly, and violence possibly, has a logical place. Only the most rigorous pacifist would say Hungarian "extremists" threw petrol bombs at Russian tanks. We recognise that these people were fighting for something we sympathise with, and which they felt could not be defended by other means.
>
> So far in Wales we have been talking as if there were a handful of people practising or advocating violence who constituted a wholly isolated current of thought, and had no general significance... Nationalists are painted as "fascists", involved in what are considered to be "petty squabbles" compared to Vietnam or Czechoslovakia. The deaths at the investiture were treated as an obscure incident in the English press.
>
> How long before we start to ask whether in Wales there are not grievances so deep that they cannot be left to the electoral processes alone?
>
> The ordinary Englishman is a person of great natural tolerance. He cannot understand why there should be bombs in Wales. He is very sympathetic to the Welsh language and cannot understand what threatens it. The Welsh speaker, even when a political nationalist, has hitherto been a natural pacifist. Somewhere in between, a structure of political and economic power has arisen that makes the one man feel oppressed by the other, sometimes to the point of taking violent action.

Ned Thomas does finally conclude that 'the hopeful course for an honest Welshman is to back the non-violent civil disobedience campaigns' but also suggests, through this quote from Dr Bobi Jones, poet and former professor in Welsh at UCW, Aberystwyth, that those who are not militant, or have done nothing, must also accept some responsibility for the young deaths in 1969:

I am a nationalist of the pen, an armchair pacifist. I do not
believe that violence is right... No, I don't agree with these lads...
But everyone who has in the least assisted in the psychological
and material subjection of Wales is responsible for their deaths.
Everyone who has been indifferent is responsible. Everyone who
supported the great circus at Caernarfon is responsible. And
everyone who has ever worked to free Wales from her servility is
responsible. In the midst of our constitutional comforts let us not
lose the humanity to see the immeasurable and terrible difference
between ourselves and those who risk – and lose – their lives.

Saunders Lewis, one of the founders and long-term president
of Plaid Cymru, was also an advocate of non-violence, but was
prepared for a more bitter struggle than the constitutional
one.

And so history has proved him right. It took ten years of
wilful protest by the Welsh Language Society to achieve a
bilingual policy towards road signs and official forms in Wales,
and a hunger strike by Gwynfor Evans before Maggie Thatcher
finally agreed to the commencement of the Welsh-language TV
channel, S4C, in 1982. The latter event occurred during the
build-up to the 1984–5 miners' strike, which in Wales broadened
into a powerful national movement involving trade unions,
political parties, churches and the Welsh Language Society. One
wonders what would have been the consequences if Gwynfor
Evans had been allowed to die. This was Mrs Thatcher's first
(and last?) political U-turn.

However, there were also more violent protests, in the
1960s, mainly by *Mudiad Amddiffyn Cymru* (Movement for the
Defence of Wales or MAC), who sabotaged water pipelines,
government offices and the Prince of Wales's1969 investiture,
and by a 1979 offshoot, *Meibion Glyndŵr* (Sons of Glyndŵr),
blamed by police for more than 200 arson attacks on English
holiday homes in Wales.

These more violent episodes in recent Welsh history,
relegated to the sidelines by more conventional historians,
have been extensively researched by former *Western Mail*

editor, John Humphries, in his book, *Freedom Fighters: Wales's Forgotten 'War', 1963–1993*.

In it, he considers to what extent such direct action helped shape a political environment in which the governing classes became more receptive to Welsh aspirations: 'What impact the insurgency had on the devolution process that eventually delivered an Assembly Government will always be contested by those who marginalise these attacks as an isolated stain on the Welsh national character. But no one can deny that devolutionary change did follow. At the very least the part played by the insurgents in Wales's "forgotten war" is bound up in the notion that one man's freedom fighter is another's terrorist... [and] far from being isolated acts... [these] were milestones in a 30-year insurgency.'

The last 50 years have seen considerable protest in the name of Welsh language, culture and identity (not all related to nationalism), and many key historical events occurred during Dai Daniel's early and teenage years in the 1960s and 1970s. Via such writers as Fishlock and Ned Thomas, these events entered Dai's consciousness and contributed to the development of his own Welsh identity.

The first series of events to arouse the latent desire of the Welsh to defend their identity was the indiscriminate use of Welsh land and resources to meet the material needs of the rest of the country.

In 1936 an RAF bombing school was sited at Penyberth on the Llŷn Peninsula after various English sites had been abandoned following objections. In protest, Saunders Lewis, D J Williams and the Reverend Lewis Valentine burnt down the aircraft sheds and then gave themselves up, claiming moral right on their side.

The jury at Caernarfon failed to agree on a verdict, and the case was transferred to the Old Bailey in London, where the accused were found guilty and sentenced.

Ned Thomas writes: 'This is always the trouble; there are two nations, there are two cultures... A government decision can be presented as democratic despite the protest of all shades of Welsh opinion, so long as the unit is thought of as the UK. Even if Welsh MPs resist... they are merely a handful in the House of Commons. The leaders of any protest are presented to everyone, including the Welsh people, as a few politically-motivated fanatics; this is a pattern that has often been seen in colonial territories.'

But the most publicised indication, a kind of landmark, that the values of Wales were in danger and were meaningless to the authorities in England, was the drowning of Tryweryn in 1957.

Trevor Fishlock comments: 'The corporation of Liverpool, with measured arrogance, and without consulting anyone involved, announced that it would have the valley as a reservoir... [yet] the city was getting all it needed for domestic purposes... Tryweryn water was wanted for industrial expansion and for re-sale at a profit.'

In the valley, the village of Capel Celyn, in the Penllyn district, was the home of traditional Welsh *penillion* singing. 'An obscure settlement, but a precious and largely unspoiled nugget of Welsh values.'

There were bomb attacks on water pipelines, and a defence committee incorporating trade unions, religious organisations and Welsh MPs was formed. Wales united as never before.

But the Bill was passed by the House of Lords, with Mr Geoffrey Lawrence arguing that, 'Liverpool Corporation have to take the constitution as they find it. There is no separate Welsh government. There is no separate demarcation of Wales from England from the point of view of water supplies.'

The next major reservoir scheme, in the Clywedog Valley, near Llanidloes, was also passed, but while homes were lost, it did not drown a village.

Then, in 1970, a milestone was achieved. The drowning of the Dulas valley, south of Llanidloes, by the Severn River Authority was rejected. It was, literally, blocked by protesters who appeared on the road whenever surveyors appeared.

There was now a statutory Secretary of State for Wales, and the inspector conducting the inquiry noted that the defence based their case on the assurance given by Labour's first Secretary of State, Mr Cledwyn Hughes, that he would not agree to the development of sites which involved the drowning of villages.

The Welsh countryside has also been ravished by centuries of industrialisation, with its associated disasters, the most infamous being at Aberfan in 1966, when a colliery waste tip collapsed on a school, killing 144, of whom 116 were children. There was outrage when the National Coal Board and the Treasury refused to accept full financial responsibility for the disaster, obliging the Disaster Fund to contribute to the removal of the remaining Aberfan tips.

John Barnard Jenkins of *Mudiad Amddiffyn Cymru* had spent time in Aberfan, and had been traumatised by the disaster.

The movement, MAC, was the only really serious militant threat to emerge over the last century, certainly compared to the 'toy soldiers' of the Free Wales Army. It was originally formed in 1963 by Gwynedd farmer Owain Williams and two accomplices, with the intention of sabotaging Tryweryn.

In 1966 six nationalist activists planted a bomb on the site of the new Clywedog Reservoir, delaying the completion of the dam for six months. No one has ever been arrested.

MAC was resuscitated by John Jenkins in 1967 who, writes John Humphries, orchestrated a campaign of sabotage that came very close to persuading Prime Minister Harold Wilson to advise Buckingham Palace to cancel the investiture of the Prince of Wales at Caernarfon Castle, an event widely regarded as a manifestation of Welsh submission to England.

Jenkins was the bomb-maker and operations director. A non-Welsh speaker, he remained unsuspected for a long time because he was actually a serving sergeant in the British Army, which he used as a cover for his bomb-making operations. He was at the very heart of the celebrations, part of the Royal Army Dental Corps assigned to look after the teeth of the 2,500 troops on ceremonial duty in Caernarfon.

According to John Humphries, four MAC cells penetrated the security shield, planting bombs at Caernarfon (two), Holyhead and Abergele. The last exploded prematurely, killing two insurgents as they assembled their bomb close to the railway line along which the train carrying the royal family was due to pass. As a result the police intensified their investigation, helped by a man who had been given a bomb by Jenkins, but now thought that matters had gone too far. Jenkins was subsequently caught and, after pleading guilty to eight charges, was jailed for ten years.

Those who escaped detection retreated underground to re-emerge in 1979 in the aftermath of the referendum defeat with a new target: the thousands of holiday homes blamed for swamping Welsh culture and identity. John Humphries suggests that, although the arsonists who torched more than 200 holiday homes did so in the name of *Meibion Glyndŵr*, those who instigated what became a ten-year campaign are thought to have had their roots in the earlier insurgency.

The less violent protests of the last half century related mainly to the use and hence preservation of the Welsh language.

The Beasley family from Llangennech, near Llanelli, refused their rate demands for eight years from 1952 to 1960 because they weren't made available in Welsh. They were taken to court a dozen times, demanded proceedings in Welsh, had the bailiffs carry their furniture away three times, and after eight years obtained a bilingual rate demand.

To the newspapers this was a 'petty squabble' but Ned Thomas had this to say about such squabbles: 'One of the most humiliating things for an educated Welshman is the time and energy he has to spend fighting for what should be unquestioned rights. I suppose one can take comfort from a series of petty victories over bureaucracy, even if the struggle rather demeans life. But it does not mean that there is not some bigger national consciousness trying to get out.'

The most iconic event in the fight to preserve the Welsh language was the BBC Wales Annual Radio Lecture delivered by Saunders Lewis in 1962 entitled *Tynged yr Iaith* [The fate of the language].

Motivated by his words, a group of students, mainly from Aberystwyth, founded *Cymdeithas yr Iaith Gymraeg* (The Welsh Language Society) at the Plaid Cymru summer school in Pontarddulais that year.

The society's first public protest took place in October 1962 at Pont Trefechan in Aberystwyth, during my time as a student there, where around 70 members and supporters held a sit-in, blocking road traffic for half an hour.

The society spent the next 20 years demonstrating for the cause. (And it still does.) The first campaigns had the objective of obtaining official status for the language, with calls for Welsh-language tax returns, schools, electoral forms, post office signs etc. At the beginning of the 1970s the society began a campaign for a Welsh-language radio and television service.

*Cymdeithas yr Iaith* believes in non-violent direct action, and in the course of its campaigns more than a thousand people have appeared before the courts, many receiving prison sentences, making it one of Britain's largest protest groups since the suffragettes in terms of fines and numbers in prison.

Typical actions included the painting of slogans on buildings and other minor criminal damage. The most newsworthy were the campaign of 1969 when practically every English road sign in Wales was daubed with green paint, and later, the climbing of television masts and the invading of studios in protest against the Conservative government reneging on its 1979 election promise of a separate Welsh television channel.

While the society was unrepresentative of the majority of Welsh speakers in its militancy, it was remarkable how over time it got its message across to larger numbers of people. And when the society's president, Dafydd Iwan, was imprisoned, demonstrations on his behalf involved all generations, including 20 magistrates who contributed to a fund set up to pay his fine and secure his release.

# 4

# A New Sovereignty?

IN THE ALMOST 40 years since the writings of Trevor Fishlock and Ned Thomas, the cultural and political landscape has fundamentally changed as a result of this, sometimes violent, but mainly non-violent civil disobedience.

The 1963 Welsh Language Report led to the 1967 Welsh Language Act giving Welsh equal validity in legal proceedings. It didn't become mandatory however until the Language Act of 1993, which also set up the Welsh Language Board to promote and facilitate the language across every public body. The recent 2011 Welsh Language Measure gave official status to Welsh alongside English. Welsh is now also more publicly visible, thanks partly to the Bowen Report on road signs in 1972.

Education has become increasingly taught through the medium of Welsh. All schoolchildren between the age of five and sixteen study Welsh, and there are 464 primary and 55 secondary Welsh-medium schools. Even in Cardiff, 12 per cent of primary school children are now taught in Welsh.

I mentioned earlier that the proportion speaking Welsh had declined through the 20th century from 50 per cent in 1900 to 19 per cent in 1991. The 2001 census, however, saw a reversal, with an increase to 21 per cent, or 28 per cent if you include those with more limited spoken or written knowledge. And the proportion of Welsh speakers increases to 40 per cent among five to fifteen-year-olds. One third of the population live in households with at least one Welsh speaker.

This incidentally excludes any contribution from us exiles, as Welsh speakers in England are still not asked census questions about their ability to speak the language. S4C estimated in the mid 1990s that there were 133,000 Welsh speakers in England, 50,000 of them in London.

Wales is now culturally more active. It has always had a strong amateur folk culture. The annual National Eisteddfod, attended by thousands, has been a national event linked to the *Gorsedd* of Bards since the early 19th century, although the very first eisteddfod is believed to date from 1176. Today it is the largest itinerant folk festival in the world. And the Llangollen International Eisteddfod was launched in 1947 to worldwide acclaim despite being largely ignored by the English media.

*Urdd Gobaith Cymru* (Welsh League of Youth), the world's largest youth organisation, was formed in 1922, it has 1,500 branches, 50,000 members and an annual eisteddfod all of its own.

The National Youth Orchestra was formed in 1946. This has now been followed by the National Brass Band in 1982, the National Youth Choir in 1984, National Youth Jazz Orchestra in 2001 and the National Youth Wind Orchestra in 2002.

Wales is also beginning to happen culturally on a more global scale. Cardiff has several mega-venues: the 74,500-seater Millennium Stadium, St David's Hall (venue of the Cardiff Singer of the World competition and a permanent home for the BBC Welsh National Orchestra), the Cardiff International Arena, and the Millennium Centre (a permanent home for several cultural organisations including the Welsh National Opera, the *Urdd* and the BBC Symphony Orchestra). Swansea is the home of the National Waterfront Museum and the National Swimming Complex, and Newport boasts a major arts centre.

Wales has its own National Botanic Garden in deepest Carmarthenshire, hosts the Brecon Jazz Festival, and the world-renowned Hay-on-Wye Book Festival.

It has its own vibrant pop music scene, both in terms of internationally-known groups, and the appeal of Welsh-language lyrics. Whoever would have imagined that a Welsh-language album would make the national charts? Super Furry Animals released an album, *Mwng,* in 2001 with entirely Welsh lyrics. It reached number 11 in the UK album charts, and also received critical acclaim in the US.

The Welsh Academy, *Academi*, created in 1958, relaunched in 2011 as Literature Wales, has recently completed two major works: a comprehensive Welsh–English dictionary, and an *Encyclopaedia of Wales*, with both Welsh and English versions. No longer do we have to rely on the *Encyclopaedia Britannica* which in its index, under the topic 'Wales', once merely stated 'see England'.

To some extent Wales now has its own media, divorced from any attachment to adjacent English regions. These include BBC Wales on television (the amount of Welsh programming is still a complete joke, but Cardiff has become a major production centre for networked programmes), Radio Wales/Cymru since 1977, and most important of all, the Welsh-language television channel, S4C, since 1982.

The Welsh are slowly being given more scope to make their own decisions. Cardiff was recognised as the capital city in 1955, the Welsh Office was made a Department of State in 1964, a Welsh Sports Council was established in 1974, and an Arts Council in 1994. Since 1982 the Wales Tourist Board has been given the right to market Wales outside of the UK.

Now all are funded by the Welsh Assembly Government, the executive body of the National Assembly which was created in 1999, identified as the most important of what Trevor Fishlock calls Wales's national 'building blocks'.

Major sporting events have come to Wales, helped by National Assembly funding, even if mainly as a result of the contribution of entrepreneurial and pro-active individual Welshmen within the different sports. Such events have included the 1999 Rugby World Cup, golf's Ryder Cup at Celtic Manor in 2010, and a first staging of an England cricket test match versus Australia. The governing body is, after all, called the England and Wales Cricket Board.

Reading the writings of Trevor Fishlock and Ned Thomas for the first time, almost 40 years after they were published, I have been struck by two underlying thoughts. Firstly, how little of the events on which they focused entered my consciousness at the time. This was partly through the lack of coverage given to them by the English media, and partly through a sense of how unimportant Wales seemed in the scheme of things which this indoctrination had instilled in me.

Secondly, I am now filled with admiration for how much such a small minority of activists, both inside and outside the corridors of power, have achieved in such a short period of our history.

Dai Daniel, having continued to keep abreast of the Welsh political and cultural environment to a far greater than myself, feels that 'the biggest fight is yet to come'.

The battle is still to be won both in terms of language and the media.

The Welsh Language Act of 1993 declared that Welsh should be treated on an equal basis with English in the public domain, but did not include areas such as the private business and voluntary sectors, both seen as principal areas of social communication in modern Wales. *Cymdeithas yr Iaith Gymraeg* also argued that the Act fell short of what was needed, and that lack of official status meant that the Welsh language was missing out on many crucial European grants. It called for Welsh and English to be declared official languages in Wales.

Within the society, the *Grŵp Deddf Iaith Newydd* (New Welsh Language Act Group) was involved in the demand for a new Welsh Language Act, and new Assembly approval was given in December 2010 to a Welsh Language Measure recognizing Welsh as an official language in both public and private matters, with Royal Approval following in February 2011. Bethan Williams, chair of *Cymdeithas yr Iaith*, still claims however that Welsh does not have official status in all aspects of our lives.

Education through the medium of the Welsh language is

available in most areas of Wales in the secondary and primary stage of school education, but the *Grŵp Addysg* (Education Group) is demanding massive expansion in the availability of further (college) and higher (university) education in Welsh. *Cymdeithas* is also pressing for more politicians to use Welsh in the chamber of the National Assembly for Wales, and its *Cymru 2020* (Wales 2020) campaign hopes 'to secure the future of the language' against what it sees as possible decline by 2020.

Adopting a more physical level of protest, on 24 July 2004, Radio Carmarthenshire's studios, five weeks after launch, were invaded by eleven activists from the society. *Cymdeithas* claimed that fifty per cent of the population of Carmarthenshire spoke Welsh as a first language, but less than five per cent of Radio Carmarthenshire's output was in Welsh. As a result of complaints and pressure, the Ofcom watchdog warned the station that any further claims that it was not conforming to the licence agreement would result in severe reprimands.

Even more aggressive activity has been orchestrated by *Cymuned* (Community), a pressure group campaigning on behalf of local communities in Wales, particularly, but not exclusively, Welsh-speaking and rural ones, which are perceived to be under threat from demographic change.

This includes protests outside estate agents in England selling second homes in Wales to English people, protests against Welsh train company Arriva Trains for its lack of use of the Welsh language on its services, and the travel company, Thomas Cook, for banning the use of Welsh at its Bangor branch in 2007.

Critics argue that estate agents are providing a commercial service to the Welsh people who contract them to sell their property at the best market value, and that rising houses prices is not a phenomenon confined to Wales. *Cymuned* counter-argues that there is a need to create a secondary sustainable local housing market in rural Wales, and has launched a new campaign designed to ensure that a proportion of new homes should be for locals only. Such an impetus is in any case based on planning policies already adopted in the Yorkshire Dales National Park, parts of Shropshire, Devon, the Peak District and the Lake District.

The battle, as Dai Daniel describes it, for the maintenance of our Welsh identity, is even more acute when it comes to Wales's representation in the media.

Clive Betts, a contemporary of mine at Aberystwyth, writes in 'Cambria Politico: The Political Blog', from the National Assembly press gallery: 'The failure by the London press to give any news coverage to Wales, at the same time as political power is increasingly being passed to the country, amounts to a serious failure of both the democratic and journalistic processes.'

There is no longer a Welsh edition of any London paper. A former BBC hack, Hywel Morris, a life member of the NUJ, was offered the *Daily Mail* at half price for three months. Before he started the subscription, he bought a copy, to find that there was in the 110 pages 'not a single item of Welsh interest in the news or sports section'.

Mr Morris's main complaint about the attitude of the English national newspapers is the increasing number of their stories that are ridiculously inaccurate for Wales as the Assembly's political remit expands.

Writes Clive Betts: 'By all means, print whatever you like. But get the Welsh material right. Particularly as you possess the full ability to do so.'

The situation with television is, if anything, worse.

The Institute of Welsh Affairs (IWA), founded in 1987, is an independent think-tank which acts as a bridge between public policy makers, the academic community, business and non-profit organisations. It is highly regarded in Wales and has built a track record of effective influence on a range of policies.

In 2009, it published several press releases concerned with 'Television's Crisis in Wales', announcing the fact that leading figures from Welsh cultural and political life, including the Archbishop of Wales, the National Poet of Wales, and the opera singer Bryn Terfel, had signed an open letter to the UK Government calling for a restoration of £25 million a year which is being lost to the English language in Wales.

In 2008, according to Ofcom's own figures, only one hour in every 2,081 hours broadcast in the UK was made in English for a Welsh audience. Since then the production of general programmes for Wales has declined still further with the terminal decline of ITV Wales programming, and severe cuts at BBC Wales. A consequence is that the annual value of television programming for Wales in English will have been reduced by £25 million a year by 2012.

Jon Gower, in an article in *English is a Welsh Language: Television's Crisis in Wales* (IWA, 2009), states: 'An American writer once suggested that a people that doesn't see itself on television begins to believe it doesn't exist. From a Welsh perspective, if one had to depend on UK network television for a sense of self or, let's go further, a sense of being, there would be ample room for self-doubt and anxiety. It can sometimes seem as if a mantle of invisibility has been cast over us.' And this at a time, to quote Clive Betts, when political power is increasingly being passed to the country.

John Osmond, director of IWA recalls Don Anderson, former Labour MP for Swansea East, once describing devolution as a 'mystery tour'. Mr Osmond goes on to say that 'a problem is that it remains a mystery tour for the Welsh people who, generally speaking, have no idea that there is a tour underway at all'.

And as a Welshman living in England I have even less of a clue. But thanks to the promptings of Dai Daniel, I am making more of an effort to learn.

The Welsh Assembly now has the ability to acquire more powers thanks to the Government of Wales Act of 2006 and most recently the 2011 referendum granting further law-making powers to the Assembly Government.

The 2006 Act originally created not only an executive body – the Welsh Assembly Government – which is separate from the legislative body, namely the National Assembly of Wales, but also provided a mechanism for orders in council to delegate power from Parliament to the Assembly.

In addition, a number of Whitehall departments of the Westminster Parliament were, according to John Osmond, unilaterally making English-only laws and in the process creating two jurisdictions, one for England and one for Wales. And this was happening with no formal procedures for consulting the National Assembly.

The Lord Richard Commission, set up by the Assembly a few years ago, saw this as creating a fundamental problem of split accountability – proposals initiated in one representative body and scrutinised and adopted in another. This led to the commission recommending a clean break in law making in Wales.

The 2006 Act also provided for a referendum to determine whether the people of Wales were happy to give the Assembly increased law-making powers.

And a Labour–Plaid Cymru joint administration (as opposed to a possible rainbow coalition' of Plaid, Tory and Lib-Dem members) subsequently produced a power-sharing document, *One Wales*, committing them to move towards a Welsh Parliament with full law-making powers.

Within six months they also intelligently set up an All-Wales Convention which reported in November 2009 having vigorously solicited opinion from the length and breadth of Wales, with a referendum set for 2011.

And the policies of such a Welsh government would be very sound if the views currently held by the Welsh Assembly are anything to go by.

George Monbiot reported for *The Guardian* from rural Gwynedd in the lead-up to the 2010 general election:

While radical rural politics are familiar in parts of France, Mexico and Brazil, those of us brought up in England associate the countryside with conservatism. Here in the remotest parts of Wales there's overwhelming support for policies well to the left of Labour's.

For the past few years a quiet but momentous revolution has been taking place. This has passed largely unnoticed in England reflecting the media's lack of interest in Wales. English progressives know more about the political transformation in Bolivia than the similar shift happening over the border. Perhaps this is just as well.

It was Plaid Cymru that led the attempt to impeach Tony Blair over the invasion of Iraq. It opposed the conflict in Afghanistan from the outset. It wants to scrap Trident and cancel the aircraft carrier and Eurofighter contracts. It would break up the banks, ban short selling, tax foreign exchange transactions, raise capital gains tax, raise income tax for the rich while reducing it for the poor. It would set a maximum wage and give workers seats on corporate boards.

It seeks to renationalise the railways and curb the powers of the supermarkets. It wants a living pension for everyone over 80, to raise benefits in line with average earnings and to scrap tuition fees. It would abandon ID cards, stop detaining asylum seekers and shift sentencing away from prison and towards restorative justice.

Such policies are widely held to make parties in England unelectable. But in Wales they are considered mainstream, and not just among Plaid supporters. The Labour Party in Cardiff is a different beast from the Labour Party in Westminster.

The Welsh Assembly Government, where Labour is the senior coalition partner, has stopped Sats in schools, scrapped the private finance initiative, is abandoning the internal market in the NHS, has imposed tough housing policies, helped set up a network of credit unions and, belatedly, more or less killed new opencast mining.

The manifesto Labour has just published for the Westminster vote would be a lengthy suicide note for the Assembly elections. What explains the difference?

In the event, the 2011 referendum voted by a majority of almost two to one in favour of giving the Welsh Assembly increased law-making powers. The main concern was that lack of interest would produce an unacceptably low turnout. The figure actually achieved was 35 per cent, higher in fact than the percentage of voters who voted on whether or not to have a London mayor. But the referendum was almost scuppered by the devious tactic of the No Vote campaign which refused to register itself as an official opposition, thus preventing any party from a right to free broadcasting and leafleting. As a result, public knowledge of the issues was limited, with 50 per cent claiming in an opinion poll that they possessed insufficient information to cast a vote.

Typically, the following day's *Daily Mail* neglected to give any coverage at all to the event.

It really is about time the Welsh people realised how little interest London has in Welsh views and requirements, how little we have benefited from a UK government in the past, and how we ought now to have a go at running our country for ourselves.

It is unfortunate that it is in the Welsh psyche to be very suspicious of any attempts by any power to increase its authority and to believe that such power is always motivated by self-interest.

The Welsh much prefer debate by committee. John Winterson Richards in his *Xenophobe's Guide to the Welsh* writes:

> Why this nation of free-spirited individualists has such a
> reverence for the committee can perhaps be put down to that
> part of every Welshman which enjoys formality and ceremony.
> Welsh committees are nothing if not formal... Business at Welsh
> committees, however insignificant and pointless it may be, and
> however violent the debates might get, must be conducted strictly
> by the book.

Unfortunately 'the book' in this instance insists that as a Welsh exile I have no say in the matter.

Lord Garel-Jones, an ex-Tory minister who was born in Wales but has lived in England and Spain since he was six, has handed in a submission to the convention signed by eminent Welsh people living in England, claiming that people of Welsh descent around the world should have a vote in any referendum on more powers for the Assembly.

He says that this shouldn't necessarily include those thousands of Welsh decent who live in southern Argentina, but certainly Welsh UK residents should surely have a say in how that part of the country in which they were born is governed? If Wales became independent, anyone with a Welsh passport would be able to vote in the Principality. Theoretically however independence would also mean less information about Wales being available in the public domain in England, but as this is already virtually nil, the issue is irrelevant. The 2001 census did not even allow Welsh exiles living in England to record their ethnicity, let alone their ability to speak the Welsh language.

Yet great strides have still been made in the last 50 years, and I will leave the last word to John Osmond of the IWA who writes: 'It is a striking testimony on how far the Welsh political establishment has been transformed in recent years, that a piece of graffiti designed to ignite political protest against a British government trampling over Welsh interests has been awarded a £30,000 Welsh Assembly Government grant. I refer of course to the "writing on the wall" on the A487 roadside a few miles south of Aberystwyth near Llanrhystud.'

Initially painted in white as *Cofiwch Tryweryn* (Remember Tryweryn) in 1963 or thereabouts, it recalls the campaign to prevent the flooding of the valley to supply water to Liverpool. It has subsequently been recrafted many times until today's image has the words *Cofiwch Dryweryn* in red on a white background complete with the *Cymdeithas yr Iaith*'s dragon tongue symbol underneath.

Now Llanrhystud Community Council has launched an

appeal to raise £80,000 to buy the wall and the land around it to preserve the landmark. The appeal has been kick-started by the £30,000 Assembly Government contribution handed over by Heritage Minister Alun Ffred Jones at the 2009 Bala Eisteddfod.

Llanrhystud Council observes: 'The flooding of the valley became a turning point in the history of Wales, convincing Welsh people that they must have the right to govern their own affairs.'

But given the strange relationship between politics and the Welsh, a final ironic scenario, writes John Osmond, is painted by Morgan Parry, chair of *Cynnal Cymru* (the Sustainable Development Forum for Wales) in the IWA's latest publication *Wales in 2050: A View from the Future.*

Looking back from 2050, he recalls that in 2015 there was a massive protest against a demand from the City of London for a new dam in the Elan Valley. Later that year a referendum on full law-making powers for the Assembly was successful, mainly because of the English demands for Welsh water. However, a few years later, 'Although the Government in Cardiff had the power to say no, they were offered good money by the private water companies that wanted to build the dam and sell water at a profit to Londoners. A deal was agreed, and construction began.'

5

# I never stop telling people I'm Welsh

IN HIS LATE teens and early adulthood, Dai Daniel went through a period when his Welshness was almost a solitary intellectual pursuit. He developed a passion for Welsh history, through reading authors like Trevor Fishlock and Ned Thomas. Although he would discuss with anyone the key political issues, boring his English friends with readings from *The Welsh Extremist*.

Ties with Glanaman weakened as an uncle died, an aunt moved to Caerphilly, and his grandmother came to live with them in London as her health deteriorated in the latter years of her life.

Chapel attendance became less frequent, although he would sometimes go with his father to Sunday morning service followed by a drink with West Indian Baptist (Willesden was Methodist) and Irish Catholic friends at the 'interdenominational' Spotted Dog pub in Willesden. After his father passed away, he would occasionally take his mother, and was always made to feel very welcome, a part of the Welsh extended family.

Dai then went off to university in Hull, subsequently taking a couple of years off to travel, spending some of the time in a kibbutz in Israel.

Returning to London 'skint', he took six months to find employment in the deep recession of 1982, regarding himself though, as 'one of the lucky ones'.

He met his wife, Jackie, at a party in Southgate. Her father was English, and although one side of her mother's family were originally from south Wales, her mother always thought of herself as a Gloucestershire girl.

He sees it as his duty to make his children aware of his background, but feels it's up to them whether they want to be a part of it or not. He just hopes he hasn't overdone the pressure.

His daughters and wife are not particularly interested either way, regarding themselves as English if pushed. The girls, he thinks, are more into LA rappers and West Coast grunge metal than anything Welsh or English.

His twin boys, true to form however, do support Wales, certainly in rugby, and possibly even in football versus England.

Dai has plans to take his family on a visit to Glanaman, the first for 'donkey's years'. His twin sons in particular want to see what their father got up to as a kid.

In recent years he has found himself wanting to become part of a larger Welsh circle rather than exist as an isolated 'Taff'. He made the decision to learn Welsh 'properly' after years of declining use. He has met up with his old chapel friends, and the London Welsh Centre was chosen as the obvious place to meet for a drink. He remembers, in his youth, the centre was 'massive', always paying a visit there when friends and family were up in London.

His return to the centre resulted in him enrolling as a Welsh learner, much to the delight of his mother, and he has continued to do so for the last six years. I am now filled with envy as he fluently converses with Welsh speakers in the bar, consciously changing from his natural north London accent to do so.

Dai has also become actively involved in the centre, including editing its full-colour quarterly members' magazine: not a simple task. And as a member of the entertainment committee, led by marketing man David Johnson and actor

Fraser Cains, he is fully occupied with generating activities to raise the much-needed funds to keep the centre alive. The centre is fast becoming a showcase for Welsh talent in London, encompassing contemporary rock and pop gigs fronted by Radio One DJ, Huw Stephens, including major Welsh bands such as *Yr Ods, Colorama* and *Brigyn,* Friday night *Clwb Comedi* sessions, sell-out concerts of folk legends Meic Stevens and Dafydd Iwan, plus more esoteric book launches and poetry readings. It is also becoming the place in London to watch Welsh rugby matches, if you are not lucky enough to have a ticket for the game.

Dai feels very Welsh, and exhibits typically Welsh characteristics. When he is in Wales he is very conscious of the classlessness of its society: 'English people in general always aspire to be, or claim to be, middle class. Even if they are not well educated, or don't have a lot of money, they bust a gut to make you believe they are middle class. In Wales, it's the exact opposite (apart from the landed gentry). Even if they've made good, with entrepreneurial skills, they see themselves as more working class. It's not just about money, or a big house, it's about shared values, community, all things bound up in that class. Even if you have more money, you don't detach yourself from working class values.' Dai has cousins who have 'earned a few bob', but are still 'working class at heart'.

It also 'gets right up his nose' that Wales doesn't get the credit it deserves for its history and achievements. This is not having 'a chip on his shoulder' but a genuine desire for deserved recognition. He is probably more conscious than me of the invisibility of Wales and things Welsh in and on the British media. I will gripe about the almost non-existent coverage of the Magners League in the sports press. Dai will also question why the only soaps on network television feature London and the north of England; why there are few 'Taffs' in any drama productions apart from the archetypical village idiot; and why the character of Inspector Morse's *Lewis* has been translated from his original portrayal as a Welshman in print to being English on the television screen.

Why have the really successful Welsh comedy series *High Hopes* and drama series *Belonging* not been given exposure on network television? Why has the historical reality programme *Life in the Coal House* only achieved this in its third series? Dai's list is endless.

In keeping with his heroes of the 1960s and 1970s, who gave up so much to defend their Welsh language and culture, Dai has never forgotten his Welshness.

He has raised my consciousness of the last 50 years of Welsh history, plus the more recent activities of *Meibion Glyndŵr* and *Cymuned*. He has introduced me to the wonderful writings of Trevor Fishlock, Ned Thomas and John Osmond, and made me even more aware of how important it is to preserve our Welshness.

He also always feels the need to explain what being Welsh is about to foreigners. He has always had to stick up for being Welsh, on the kibbutz and, as he puts it, in all the drinking holes of Europe and Africa. He recalls recently explaining his nationality to two such Dutch acquaintances. 'It's not the be-all or end-all, but I have never stopped telling people I am Welsh.'

In parallel, wherever he has travelled, he has sought out fellow Welshmen. When living in Jerusalem with an Irish Roman Catholic girl, he found himself one day surrounded by Welsh visitors from the Amman Valley. He introduced himself to the preacher (*y pregethwr*), who just happened to know his mother's cousin, the preacher at Willesden.

As Dai puts it: 'Doesn't matter where you go in the world, you will always find Taffs.' And I bet he's related to most of them.

# Tony Fielden

1

## *Sais* in Colwyn Bay

I FIRST APPROACHED Tony Fielden about the possibility of adding his biography to this book because I believed him to be a *Gog* (north Walian) and therefore an interesting addition in my search for views on Welshness.

The mistake was easily made as I first encountered him as a fellow drinker in the Radlett Men's Club, defending the virtues of the Welsh rugby team against all and sundry. Such was the resoluteness with which he defended his corner he more often than not received a fair amount of flack in return, despite the fact that there were no rugby followers in the club to appreciate the finer points of his analysis.

Not that the debates continued for any length of time as Tony is incapable of staying in one place for long, unless that is, his mobile goes off in the meantime, which it frequently does. An active, energetic man, he runs most days and last year cycled the 50-plus miles from his daughter's house in Eton back to Radlett. He is also Radlett's over-60s squash champion.

When I finally tied him down to have a lengthier chat I discovered that, while being born and bred in Colwyn Bay on the north Wales coast, his parents actually hailed from Rochdale in Lancashire. So he was, in fact, first generation *Sais* (English).

This has turned out to be an even more interesting

variant in my search for views on Welshness, dovetailing nicely with the views of Dai Daniel, of Welsh descent but born in England.

The Fieldens were a long-established Rochdale family, with John Fielden, a social reformer of the 1830s, being the brains behind the Shaftesbury Factory Act which limited the working day to ten hours per day.

Tony's father was a junior manager in a dye factory, later to work in a bomb making factory during the Second World War. By the end of the war he had the desire to get out of 'the smoke' and run his own business. He bought a kiosk on the beach at Colwyn Bay, in pole position next to the pier, later expanding into the Miami Coffee Bar, which in the manner of *Happy Days* was the 'in' place for sixth-formers bunking off in the 1960s. Paula Yates once worked in the kiosk, and Alun Michael, one-time Secretary of State for Wales, was a Miami regular.

Colwyn Bay itself was a fairly anglicised holiday resort, at one time attracting hordes of factory workers from the north and midlands of England each summer.

All the seaside resorts of the north Wales coast developed with the advent of tourism in the latter part of the 18th century. They then saw real growth as Wales was opened up by the coming of the railways after 1850, this despite its dirty sea water feeding out of the Mersey estuary.

Several large estates were given over to accommodating thousands of visitors: Llandudno was developed by Baron Mostyn on his Gloddaith estate, Colwyn Bay by the owners of the Pwllycrochan estate. The growth of Rhyl, the north Wales version of Blackpool with fewer middle class tourists, was more haphazard.

With recent immigration from north-west England, Colwyn Bay has become the second largest urban area, after Wrexham, in north Wales, with a current population of 29,000. With several recent local government reorganisations, it has been, at different times, part of Denbighshire, Clwyd and now Conwy. Tony could in fact claim to have been born in three different counties.

Colwyn Bay these days is less of a seaside resort and more of a cut-price dormitory town for Liverpool, dissected, even destroyed, by the expressway that is the A55. Tony regrets its demise, remembering how its lovely shops mirrored places like Bournemouth and Torquay, to be replaced now by rows of charity shops. His old home, a semi-detached house in treelined Old Colwyn *(Hen Golwyn)*, today has multiple occupants, probably all on supplementary benefit. Yet Llandudno, just six miles away, is still 'a really nice place to go', and has become a Mecca for the elderly.

Another facet of the human geography of north Wales, is how, like south Wales, the major lines of communication flow west–east into England. So, while Cardiff in the south is now established as Wales's capital city, north Walians have for centuries looked east towards Liverpool and Manchester for their commercial and leisure focus.

In 1901, there were 265,000 Welsh-born inhabitants in England, the favourite destination being the north-west, with 87,000 inhabitants of Lancashire and Cheshire being Welsh-born. Between 1851 and 1911, Liverpool alone attracted at least 20,000 Welsh people in every decade.

John Davies points out, in his *A History of Wales*, that because of the constancy of the influx, Welsh culture flourished in the city for 60 years or more. Liverpool was the home of the first real newspaper in the Welsh language, and there were 50 Welsh chapels in the city. The Welsh National Eisteddfod was actually held there on three occasions.

The Welsh also became quite prominent in business, in the building industry in particular, and John Davies quotes Gareth Miles's claim that Liverpool produced the only well-established bourgeoisie that the Welsh nation has ever possessed, even to the extent of becoming quite versed in exploiting their own countrymen among their workers.

Tony, in his youth, found that the rail network made

Manchester far more accessible than Liverpool and, as a result, became a lifelong Manchester United fan. He still remembers coming home from school and being distraught to learn about the Munich air disaster. He is almost as vociferous in his support of United as he is a fan of the Welsh rugby team. He proudly told me that he once served Bobby Charlton at his father's ice cream kiosk, getting him to sign a plaster cast acquired by Tony to protect a football injury. Bobby's wife Norma actually hails from Old Colwyn.

North Wales has always been more of a soccer than a rugby hotbed and, over the years, the area has been an important nursery for the major professional clubs of the north-west, providing Wyn Davies, Ron Davies, Ian Rush, Michael Owen, Micky Thomas, Neville Southall and Mark Hughes, as Tony reminded me.

With such strong links with north-west England to the east, including the heavy reliance on English tourism, I have always assumed that the resorts of the northern coastline of Wales would not be heavily into the Welsh language, unlike the heartland of the language further west in Gwynedd.

However, even in the 2001 census, 23 per cent still spoke Welsh in the Colwyn electoral ward, and Tony points out that the real divide is north–south. Only a few miles inland from the coast at Colwyn Bay, in towns like Llanrwst, Denbigh and Ruthin, the Welsh language is far more prevalent. In Upper Conwy, part of the same county borough, the proportion of Welsh speakers rises to 67 per cent.

Tony studied Welsh in school, and there is now even a Welsh-medium primary school in Colwyn Bay. And while only 23 per cent speak Welsh in the area as a whole, the highest proportion of 38 per cent is to be found among ten to fourteen-year-olds.

*Yma o hyd.*

## 2

# I'm from north Wales; where else am I from?

WHAT WERE THE factors that contributed to Tony's sense of Welshness?

First of all, the family liked living there. To quote Tony, 'Father loved Colwyn Bay to bits. He would read anything about it in the paper. He was far fonder of Colwyn Bay than where he was born.'

Tony also liked the scenic north Wales environment, often going walking in Snowdonia. He remembers, when he was about 16, climbing Tryfan, with its classic pointed peak, on the shores of Llyn Ogwen, and taking on the challenge of jumping the 1.2 metre gap between Adam and Eve, the two three-metre rocks which sit astride each other on the summit.

As recently as 2007, a 32-year-old man from Oxford died on his descent from this summit, with the coroner criticising a cheap guide book for providing what was mistakenly described as 'the easy route' down. Tryfan, at 3,002 feet, is only 14th in the list of Welsh peaks higher than 3,000 feet. It is still a serious mountain.

The family also became very much part of the community of Colwyn Bay. Tony's father 'knew everybody, and everybody knew him'. Tony helped out in the Miami Coffee Bar, which his own mates shared with the boys from Rydal, the local well-known public school, without any obvious animosity.

In the summer the town was taken over by factory workers

from the north of England and the Midlands, spending their week's holiday hiding under the pier from the rain. Each town in the north of England would have its own set 'wakes week', so Tony could tell the date by, which town's inhabitants were on holiday that week, and even by, which brand of cigarettes they purchased and smoked. While serving in the shop, Tony also became expert at mimicking their different accents.

But he partly resented the presence of these holidaymakers, loving Colwyn Bay much more in the winter than the summer.

His first feelings of Welshness came when his mother encouraged him to support the Welsh rugby team as he watched Wales v Scotland on their old black and white Pye television. The star of the game was the Llanelli fullback, Terry Davies, also a boyhood hero of mine.

Sport again has proved to be a major source of national identity. Tony was sports mad and played football for his school against towns from across the whole of north Wales: Bangor, Llanrwst, Denbigh, Ruthin and Mold, giving him a great sense of belonging to the region. He later played for the Mold and Buckley town teams, and obtained his Welsh FA coaching badge at Sophia Gardens in Cardiff. His roommate was Tony Pulis, currently manager of Stoke City.

Tony is very proud of the long list of footballers from north Wales who have made it professionally, including three former First Division goalkeepers – Dai Davies, Neville Southall, Eddie Niedzwicki – who he claims all hailed from Colwyn Bay. Wikipedia disagrees with him, stating that Southall was from Llandudno, Niedzwicki from Bangor, and even suggesting that Dai Davies was born not in north but south Wales, in Glanaman in Carmarthenshire's Amman Valley. Is this a localised variant of the 'everyone has a Welsh ancestor' syndrome?

Tony also recalls with pride the now defunct Borough

United, based in nearby Llandudno Junction, playing and winning matches in the European Cup at The Racecourse in Wrexham.

All schools play football in north Wales, and the North Wales School Football Association never missed a potential prospect, especially, according to Tony, compared to his more recent experience of disorganised Watford and Hertfordshire's capacity to let local talent slip through the net.

In such a pro-active football environment Tony became a follower of the Welsh rather than the English football team, although he would support the latter he claims against any other team in the world. He is also loyal to the heritage of his parents, always keeping an eye on Rochdale's results, and acknowledging his cousin as a huge Burnley fan.

Tony's support however doesn't extend to the English rugby team. 'I suppose it's their arrogance really.' He recalls the last occasion (probably 'the very last time') that he watched Wales play England at HQ (Twickenham). He had to ask the people in the seats behind him to stop talking during the singing of the Welsh national anthem.

In keeping with most contributors to, and references employed by this book, Tony expresses the feeling that Welsh values are tied up more with education and family, more with a desire to experience life than with materialism and one-upmanship. Hence his later involvement in teaching and the development of skills in others.

He commented on my own tendency to use the word 'coll' rather than 'uni', when describing an establishment of further education, as 'a very Welsh thing to say', a typical example of Welsh understatement.

Tony was also exposed to the Welsh language. His primary school headmaster was 'Pop' Davies, a Welsh speaker, who lived 100 yards from Tony's house and whose daughter helped Tony's dad in the café during the summer holidays. As a result of 'Pop' Davies, school assemblies were held partly in Welsh as well as English.

Tony studied Welsh in school, and as a second language when a student at Bangor Normal Training College. Welsh was frequently spoken at the college, and it was here he met his wife, Andrea, a fluent Welsh speaker. Andrea's great-grandmother had actually been among the nonconformist Welsh who had emigrated to form a Welsh colony in Patagonia, only to return home later.

As an adult Tony befriended former Tottenham player, Ken Barton, and sat alongside him in the commentary box as Ken did the Welsh-language broadcasts when Wales played at Wrexham. He was there the afternoon Wales beat England 4–1.

Tony also recalls lots of Welsh singing in the pubs and on the coach driving back overnight from college sports fixtures in south Wales.

Tony believes the English always think that Wales is a long way away from England, but on the contrary have no concept of how much more difficult it is to travel within Wales, from north to south. He speaks of David Lloyd George, when MP for Caernarvon Boroughs in north Wales, travelling via London by train to visit his daughter Megan, MP for Carmarthen in the south.

Even in my own childhood, my father always considered all railway lines led to London, with London being 'up line' and Llanelli and all stations, whether in south or north Wales, being 'down line'.

Tony is conscious of the Welsh characteristic of talking themselves down. In his youth it wasn't the 'in' thing to speak Welsh. He remembers even his Welsh-speaking father-in-law 'taking the mick' out of the parochialism of the Welsh nationalists, whom he referred to as *y werin* which roughly translates as 'the peasants'. There is a strange dichotomy between the Welsh love of debate and argument, and their inability to show any interest in politics unless there is a major social cause which needs fighting.

Tony feels that Welsh has more status now, and that

Welshness would be diminished without its language. He's not about to relearn it however, finding Portuguese enough and more useful for his frequent sojourns to his family's holiday home.

In politics Tony is influenced more by people than policies. Typically Welsh, he is sceptical about the Welsh Assembly, not sure how well the money is being spent, but he sees the need for a stronger Welsh identity.

And his heart is in Wales. He speaks fondly of drinking Brains dark in the Old Arcade in Cardiff on international days, watching the now deceased Emlyn Hughes playing crib with the locals by the fireplace underneath a famous old Welsh verse which adorns the wall.

*To be born in Wales*
*Not with a silver spoon in your mouth,*
*But, with music in your blood*
*And with poetry in your soul,*
*Is a privilege indeed.*

# 3

# A Welsh Enthusiasm for Education

TONY'S CHARACTER BRINGS to mind Ursula, a Welsh exile in Japan, whom American Pamela Petro met on her *Travels in an Old Tongue: Touring the World Speaking Welsh*. A non-Welsh speaker with a Welsh father, an Austrian mother and a Japanese husband, she was discouraged from speaking both Welsh and German. Ursula felt cheated out of two of her three birthright languages, so she learnt Japanese instead, and enthusiastically embraced Japanese culture. Her 'sheer vitality and breadth of interests' Pamela Petro likened to 'a typhoon'.

At the same time Ursula remained confident in her Welshness, telling anyone who was prepared to listen, in her broad south Wales accent, that she was Welsh. She claimed that enthusiasm was what being Welsh was all about. It was her way of speaking Welsh to Pamela – that they communicated in English was beside the point.

It was the same with Tony's enthusiasm for education.

He was keen initially to stay in Wales, so he did his teacher's training at Bangor Normal College, followed by a spell as a primary school teacher in Connah's Quay.

He then spent a year acquiring an advanced diploma in physical education from Leeds Carnegie College. His athletics coach was Ron Pickering and alumni include Brendan Foster and Austin Healey. This was followed by four years as head of PE at Chester City Grammar School.

Whatever post Tony held he found time to undertake further

part-time study. While at Chester, he studied for a University of Wales Bachelor of Education in vocational training at Wrexham.

Then, while lecturing in liberal studies at Widnes Further Education College, he undertook a master's degree in outdoor education, which saw him head off, with the family in tow, to teach climbing, skiing and orienteering at an American international school above the snow line in the Swiss Alps.

He returned to a senior lecturer's post in the Liverpool district of Old Swan. This was a 'job for life', but Tony saw more scope and value in vocational training, and moved to help set up a Business Training Centre in Birkenhead, teaching IT and life skills to deprived, unemployed 16- to 18-year-olds. This was in the aftermath of the Toxteth riots, and was an initiative of Michael Heseltine, in his capacity as Minister for Merseyside. After 12 months, 51 out of 57 students had obtained employment, and when recently surfing the net, Tony found that several of his former pupils now held major high-powered positions in business.

He was head-hunted by British Oxygen (BOC) to see if he could achieve similar results on a larger scale in London. Obtaining the post involved sixteen interviews, three psychometric tests plus a final interview in Manhattan.

In the 1980s, qualifications always had to precede a career path. To combat a perceived skills shortage, this new concept involved recruiting those who had a desire and an aptitude rather than qualifications to get into IT.

They advertised in the *Evening Standard*, and Tony even went on the *Jimmy Young Show*, guaranteeing a job with every student place. One hundred and eighty were taken on, and nine months later, all had jobs.

Tony wrote to Maggie Thatcher telling her about the scheme. And after a second attempt, she was persuaded to visit the centre in Hammersmith to meet the students.

Subsequently Tony started his own IT learning company based in Radlett. The company were distributors of a Microsoftcredited desktop certification used by schools and businesses all over the UK, and also in Spain.

Now in retirement he is still keen to teach, taking primary school kids from the rough area of west Watford in tag rugby, even winning a 2008 Saracens-sponsored tournament involving 600 schools. The bureaucracy of risk assessment and policy dictates however almost drove him crazy, so he has since turned his attention to just cricket coaching with Radlett Cricket Club.

# 4

# Preserving Welshness across the Generations

TONY'S MOVE TO London has seen him and his family settle in Radlett. In typical fashion, they have become involved in the community, in particular the cricket, rugby and squash clubs. Tony's son Nick captained the Radlett cricket team to the *Evening Standard* Trophy at the Oval in 2003. His South African son-in-law also played for Radlett having previously been on Middlesex's books. And Tony's five- and six-year-old grandsons are already showing good style at the crease.

But Tony feels an exile, finding Radlett 'too much about flash cars and where you go on holidays', in sharp contrast to the Welsh and their lack of interest in things material, and a greater value placed on the family and education.

As we spoke, a Mercedes coupé sped past, driven by an ageing beauty, with a number plate spelling out the word *BLONDIE*. Enough said.

Settling in England, it is impossible to over-emphasise the importance of one's close family in the preservation of Welshness. And Tony's family has become both more or less Welsh.

Tony's wife, Andrea, is a Welsh speaker. His son, born in Chester, claims jokingly to have been 'brainwashed' into supporting all teams Welsh. Tony still recalls his son's Welsh rugby baptism at the 1988 England game at Twickenham, getting into the ground with one ticket between them. This was the last time, until 2009, that Wales won at 'HQ', going on in the same year to take the Triple Crown, and missing out on the Grand Slam against France by just a single score.

Nick is a cricket fanatic, and the best university options for the sport happened to be Durham and Swansea. At Swansea, Nick met his wife Nerys, a fluent Welsh speaker from Newtown in mid Wales, who undertook all her secondary education and A levels through the medium of Welsh.

Tony's wife Andrea's grasp of the Welsh language is now a little rusty, but she and Nerys do on occasions converse in God's language, whenever they need to keep a secret.

Nerys and Nick have two young children, recently increased to three, and Nerys has indicated to me an interest in the Welsh-language school in Stonebridge, north London, for the offspring. She recalls two sisters from that school joining her primary class when she was a child and speaking 'absolutely perfect Welsh'. No hint of a missed mutation or the use of an English word.

But with Stonebridge a three-quarters of an hour drive away, logistically this is probably little more than a pipe dream. On the other hand, moving back to mid Wales is also not totally out of the question. Nick, she claims, would not be unhappy with such a move.

But Nick and Nerys are part of a settled family in Radlett, with all members of the family happily popping in to see each other at any time. Nerys thinks 'it's lovely... a really nice family'.

A community spirit has grown up around Radlett Cricket Club, Radlett Tennis and Squash Club, Tabard Rugby Club and Porters Park Golf Club, with the Fieldens very much involved. They are quite a sporting family. And Radlett, for its size, boasts a more active sporting environment than most, certainly more than I found previously in either Rickmansworth or Bushey, both also in Hertfordshire.

This sense of community is not as all-encompassing as Nerys found village life in mid Wales. Radlett as a village still has many disparate elements, particularly of a religious nature. It nevertheless has this small sporting enclave within the greater community.

And, as always, one's children have to be encouraged to become active participants in the community in which they find themselves, Welsh or otherwise. The Welsh have never been one for ghettos.

Nick's sister, Jane, also studied at Swansea University, but probably sees herself as less Welsh than Nick, despite donning a Welsh rugby shirt in support of the national team, and playing lacrosse for the Welsh universities.

She has married a die-hard South African, brought up both in Reading and South Africa. Son Ben has been seen wearing a South African rugby shirt, despite Nick and Nerys offering the bribe of a Welsh jersey as a birthday present. Living in Windsor, Ben has also shown a club rugby allegiance to Harlequins, and even receives mini-rugby tuition from New Zealanders Zinzan Brooke and Sean Fitzpatrick.

Ben calls his South African grandparents *Ouma* and *Oupa* (Afrikaans), and his Welsh grandparents *Nain* and *Taid* (north Wales Welsh). At least not an English name in sight!

It will be interesting to see whether and how the Fielden family preserves its Welshness across the generations. There is still work to be done.

# The Next Generation

## Nerys

## Clare

## Heinke

The older generation of first-language Welsh speakers, such as Alan Rees's family in Glanaman, saw Welsh as the language of everyday, plus the major tenet of a broad 'peasant' based culture. But to get on in life and the world, they still felt you needed English. And the sovereignty of the Welsh nation was of far less importance than the broader socialist issues closer to the hearts of such Welsh communities.

Growing up in the 1950s in slightly more urbanised Llanelli, and with only one Welsh-speaking parent, Welsh was even less relevant to progressing in life. In the aftermath of the Second World War, there was much more stress placed on Britishness, supported as it was by the growth of television as the new, London and English-language dominated mass medium – with the coronation of Queen Elizabeth II being the major catalyst encouraging families to acquire the new technology.

Thirty years on, in the Wales of the 1980s, thanks to the partisan efforts of a very vocal minority, Welsh had begun to acquire a degree of status. Even in the fairly anglicised Severn Valley, in mid Wales, Tony Fielden's daughter-in-law, Nerys, and her two siblings, would be encouraged to study through the medium of Welsh by her Welsh-speaking, north Walian father, with both parents also recognising the new economic and social benefits of a degree of fluency in the Welsh language.

But such fluency, whilst it matters, is of less value to Welsh exiles living in England. Regional Welsh television isn't accessible terrestrially; there is no Welsh coverage in the London newspapers, and the chapels which once formed the nucleus of a Welsh support group in London are rapidly disappearing. Even the Welsh rugby team, so long a focus of national pride, seems to be in terminal decline since 1980.

Nerys, now domiciled in England, feels guilty about how difficult it is to introduce the Welsh language to her young family, despite the fact that her husband and in-laws are Welsh connected.

Yet there is evidence from my Welsh learners' group that, among both non-Welsh-speaking exiles and first generation

Welsh, there is an increasing desire to learn Welsh to connect with their roots. Being Welsh is now much more an 'in' thing. One such learner (*dysgwr Cymraeg*) is Clare, a 27-year-old barrister brought up in north Staffordshire with an Essex mother and a non-Welsh-speaking Welsh father. Perhaps one day my son Gareth will be so motivated? (I wish.)

Foreign immigrants seem also keen to embrace what Welsh culture has to offer. In our Welsh learners' group is Heinke, a German girl who was so taken by the friendliness and caring nature of the Welsh during her stay as a registrar in Morriston Hospital that, although now seconded to the Royal Free Hospital in Hampstead, she is homesick for the Swansea Uplands. She has a Welsh boyfriend from Lampeter, she has been learning Welsh for several years (spoken with a noticeable west Wales accent) and, the greatest accolade of all, she has even fallen in love with rugby and become a Scarlets season ticket holder.

# Nerys

TONY FIELDEN'S DAUGHTER-IN-LAW, Nerys, was brought up in Abermule, a little village to the east of Newtown in the fairly anglicised Severn Valley, not far from the border with England. Apart from one near-neighbour, she says there were hardly any Welsh speakers in the village.

But in the Wales of the early 1980s, Welsh was being promoted far more heavily than in my childhood, every area had its Welsh-language school, and there were more and more jobs for which it was advantageous to be able to speak Welsh.

And Nerys's father was keen, as a proud north Walian, the son of a quarryman from Caernarfon, a first language Welsh speaker, and a Plaid Cymru voter, that all three of his offspring should attend a Welsh-language school and learn to speak properly in Welsh.

He grew up speaking only Welsh until well into his teens, yet ironically, and so typical of his generation, he qualified to teach English and drama, even holding teaching posts in Newcastle and Birmingham, where the school children used to tease him about his pronunciation of English words.

He later became a primary school adviser in mid Wales where he met Nerys's mother. She was raised in the Newtown area, in another small village, Aberhafesp, to the west of the town, but her parents were also originally from Pwllheli in north Wales. Her mother spoke Welsh, but her father didn't, so her Welsh language was more 'watered down'. She had an understanding, but was less confident in conversation. And her politics were Liberal, typical of Montgomeryshire, not Plaid Cymru.

Nerys maintains however that her mother definitely

perceived herself to be Welsh, regardless of the language. 'No way was she English!'

Nerys's dad was even more passionately Welsh, with his fervent support of the Welsh rugby team being a major component. He loved his sport. His brother also even altered their surname to the Welsh spelling of Tomos.

Nerys often wonders what her dad would now say (he died in 2000) about his grandchildren being brought up in England. She recalls how she took an age to drum up the courage to tell him about her initial move to England. He actually proved fine about it; he had after all lived there himself for a time.

One also wonders how he reacted to Nerys originally being born in Shrewsbury, to cater for any repeat of the complications Nerys's mother had encountered when giving birth to her older brother. Nerys still gets teased these days about her place of birth by colleagues at her St Alban's school. And I worry about being born a Jack?

Nerys's father always spoke to her, and her brother and sister, in Welsh, and would get annoyed with them when their Welsh wasn't as good as his, particularly when it came to missing a mutation.

Nerys recalls that 'if he spoke to you in English, you were definitely in big trouble. He always felt he couldn't tell us off in Welsh, as it was too nice a language to tell you off in.' I'm not sure the fire and brimstone Welsh nonconformist ministers in their pulpits ever exhibited similar doubts.

All three siblings went to a Welsh-language primary school in Newtown. But they spoke English to their mother and among themselves, and many of the children at the school were also from families where only one parent spoke the language, so weren't comfortable speaking Welsh all of the time. 'Oh God, we've got to speak Welsh!' they'd exclaim, when in a sort of reversal of the Welsh Not, mentioned in an earlier chapter, the teachers would reprimand the children for not speaking Welsh as opposed to English in the playground.

In fact the school had separate English and Welsh units,

and coincidentally the wife of Nerys's brother used to attend the English section, although her education did naturally incorporate some elements of Welsh.

Secondary school was different. The siblings went to the nearest Welsh-language school in Llanfair Caereinion in the next valley, travelling each day in a minibus with another family from the village, to meet up with the school bus which ran between Newtown and the school, the total journey amounting to 12 miles in each direction.

The Einion Valley (Dyffryn Banwy ac Einion) was far more Welsh-speaking, so Welsh was more naturally the language of the playground, with Nerys feeling like one of the more anglicised children at the school.

At the time Nerys begrudged having to speak and study in old-fashioned Welsh, but looking back she is really pleased she did. And a major part of this pleasure stems from the role of Welsh in the group culture of the community, with its eisteddfodau, music, drama and *cydadrodd* (group recitation).

Nerys's mam and dad were what she likes to call 'drama-type people', and they had actually first met at an eisteddfod. They weren't chapelgoers, but a lot of the school's Welsh-language activities revolved around religious festivals and carol concerts.

Nerys feels that a fundamental part of Welshness is participating in such group cultural activities, and today she misses the feeling of belonging and the community spirit that such activity engenders. In Radlett, the Fielden family are very active members of a sporting community, but this doesn't represent the whole of Radlett in the way that eisteddfodau involve the whole of Welsh-speaking Wales.

What other characteristics of the Welsh people does Nerys feel sets us apart from the English? She thinks we 'talk a lot more'. She is conscious of this on a daily basis, gossiping with the six Welsh teachers and classroom assistants who share her St Alban's school staffroom. (Or should I call it 'Taffroom?')

The passionately Welsh PE teacher, a non-Welsh speaker, greets her every morning with a *Bore da, bach* (sort of 'Good morning, love'). It must be indicative of a desire to be seen as different, that Welshmen, even from non-Welsh-speaking parts such as the Vale of Glamorgan or Gwent, are always keen to identify their Welshness with the odd *nos da* (good night) or *diolch yn fawr* (thank you very much), even though they have no intention of adopting the language on a full-time basis.

Nerys also likes to think that the Welsh are more caring, brought up as they are with a greater sense of community. She feels she doesn't have a lot of basis for this claim, except the biased voice of her dad in her ear, but she'd like to think this is the case, which is at least some indication that such attitudes are important to us Welsh.

Nerys went on to sit her A levels through the medium of Welsh prior to studying geography through the medium of English at Swansea University. (She didn't want to go to Aber because 'everyone went to Aber'.) I found it interesting and encouraging that sitting A levels in Welsh did not prove a barrier to being offered a university place to study in English, even at English universities. Nerys did however make her geography tutor aware prior to her first essay while at Swansea that this represented her very first attempt ever at a geography essay in English rather than Welsh.

At Swansea Nerys met Tony Fielden's son Nick, who she claims was very keen to impress upon her that he was genuinely Welsh. 'Exactly how Welsh are you?' she would say to him. 'Your dad's not Welsh, is he? Actually, not at all Welsh. But your mum's from Denbigh, isn't she? So that's OK.'

To her folks she would say: 'Oh no, he really is Welsh.'

But after college Nick obtained work in the London area, so he and Nerys ended up living in a flat in Radlett, close to father-in-law Tony and his family (probably for the same price as a three-bedroomed detached house in Welshpool).

Nerys talked a lot about being Welsh to Tony, and she

quickly recognised his passion for Welsh rugby. In fact the first few times they met were at rugby matches.

Nerys and Nick also announced their Welshness to the rest of Radlett by hanging the Welsh flag out of their bedroom window following a rugby success over England. Fellow regulars from the Cat and Fiddle opposite however retaliated by climbing up and 'confiscating' the emblem.

Five-year-old son Tom already sees himself as Welsh. He plays mock games of rugby in their garden, insisting on being clapped out of the house pretending to be various of his Welsh rugby heroes, and singing his own version of the Welsh national anthem, much to the amazement of the neighbours who think he's barmy.

However, when Tom hears Nerys speaking to her brother on the phone in Welsh, he gets annoyed because he can't understand what's being said. And when Nerys watches a programme on Welsh-language channel S4C, husband Nick finds it hilarious picking out the many English-sounding Welsh words. He does however tune in himself to the frequent *Clwb Rygbi* match broadcasts.

Nerys feels guilty that the children will probably not become Welsh speakers, with Welsh not being spoken by the close family, and recognising the real need for offspring to integrate into the environment in which they find themselves.

I mentioned earlier that Nerys had shown an interest in the Welsh-language school at Stonebridge, north London, having been impressed by the standard exhibited by two of its pupils who joined her primary school class during her childhood in Newtown. But Stonebridge is a good 45 minutes away from Radlett, with Nerys's own school in the opposite direction in St Albans. And such a school also comes at a financial cost.

The family are settled in Radlett, and, as Welsh-speaking Wilbur from the Mid Surrey Bowls Club once expressed to me, speaking Welsh at home to your offspring will not necessarily benefit them in an outside world which happens to be England.

So in practical and social terms a Welsh-language education may not be possible or sensible for Nerys's offspring.

Compare this situation with that of an English girl in the Gray's Inn Road learners' class who is not only learning Welsh to please her Welsh-speaking husband, but is also moving house with her family specifically to be closer to the Welsh-language school in Stonebridge.

So keen is her husband to perpetuate his family's Welshness, that he even stopped their four-year-old son from joining his friends in wearing an English football jersey to support the team during the 2010 World Cup. Herein lies the dilemma: preserving the family's Welshness while also allowing the children to relate to their environment.

The above are two scenarios. A third is to actually move back to Wales itself. This possibly remains an option for Nerys and her family. Her mother still lives in mid Wales, her brother lives and works in Welshpool, and her sister is in Swansea.

Nerys speaks Welsh to her brother, who uses the language on a daily basis in his environmental work dealing with Welsh-speaking farmers. The Welsh of Nerys's sister, is, however, 'a little rusty', at least according to Nerys, so the two girls always converse in English.

When speaking Welsh, Nerys's accent also varies, dependent upon the other party. In conversations with her brother she adopts a *Gog* (north Walian) more high-pitched delivery. Talking to her ex-college friends in Swansea she becomes a *Hwntws* (south Walian). And in mid Wales itself, the dialect can switch from north to south within a few miles.

Preserving our Welshness was never going to be easy.

# Clare

YOU DON'T HAVE to be born in Wales, or live in Wales, to feel Welsh. Clare, a 27-year-old barrister, is a Welsh learner in Gray's Inn Road, but was brought up in north Staffordshire, one of three daughters of a Welshman and a mother who came from Leigh-on-Sea in Essex.

Clare's father hails from Llanymynech, just south of Oswestry, a village situated smack bang on the border, half in England and half in Wales. I understand it has two separate local councils representing either side of the border, and, in the days of Welsh Sunday closing, a pub which literally straddled the border had one bar open and one bar shut each Sabbath. Surely the stuff of soap opera.

Clare's father went to primary school in Wales, where they used to speak Welsh once a week on a Friday morning, and then secondary school in Oswestry in England.

During her childhood he would occasionally show off his knowledge of Welsh words, which she now realises, as she is learning Welsh herself, failed to demonstrate that he could speak Welsh with any degree of fluency. He would also take the family on numerous holidays to north Wales, with countless visits to castles and Victorian schoolrooms. And naturally he supports the Welsh rugby team.

He never demanded that she see herself as Welsh, yet living fairly close to the Welsh border and her Welsh grandparents, she was exposed to a certain amount of Welshness even from an early age.

As a child Clare saw a lot of her grandparents. Being the eldest of the three daughters she would be packed off to visit them on her own, to give her parents a bit of a break. Clare isn't certain that her grandparents were fluent Welsh speakers, although her great-grandparents, whom she knew as *Nain* and *Taid*, probably did speak Welsh. Her grandparents moved to *Pant* (translates as a small valley or dingle), a Welsh-named village located in England. But their heart was in Wales, their house was called *Ael y Bryn* (translated as 'brow of the hill'), and they were members of a local Welsh Pentecostal Chapel. Clare was a frequent attendee at Sunday morning services, and her overriding memory was of singing 'Guide Me O Thou Great Redeemer' (Cwm Rhondda) on every conceivable occasion.

There were also Welsh memorabilia to be seen at the various family homes: a tapestry incorporating a Welsh dragon (*Y Ddraig Goch*), a chair bearing an inscription in Welsh, and Clare's grandparents and aunts often dropping Welsh words into their conversation.

Her sister got so excited recently that she had to phone Clare when she heard the word *'cwtch'* or *'cwtsh'* (which translates as 'hug'), a familiar expression of their aunt, being used by a character in the television programme *Gavin and Stacey*. And their grandmother would always exclaim *'mochyn'* (meaning 'pig') if the grandchildren made a mess while eating their tea.

Her dad's family always thought that being Welsh was important. As a consequence of being a minority, being Welsh seems to matter more to the Welsh, than being English does to the English. And this would be exacerbated by the English always making a point of reminding you that you were different anyway.

Clare has found it difficult to ignore her heritage. People pick up on her Welsh surname, Parry, often confusing it with Perry. Her ability to correctly pronounce Welsh place-names also doesn't go unnoticed. If arguments develop at work she is suddenly the 'Welsh mafia'. Although being Welsh, and stubborn, she is not slow to defend her corner.

She feels that things might have been different had her mother also been more strident about being English, but the situation was complicated by her mother having French ancestors, with Clare's grandfather being fluent in both French and English.

Clare feels that the birth of Scottish and Welsh assemblies has more recently generated a greater sense of nationality among the English. Her other half is becoming more proud of his Englishness and Clare has noticed the flag of St George replacing the Union Jack as the English emblem at sporting events. You have only to compare any film of the 1966 football World Cup final with any England game at the 2010 World Cup in South Africa to be instantly aware of this.

Clare always identifies herself as British. 'Strictly speaking I am English, as I was born in England, but I wouldn't volunteer English, I prefer to say British.' And her national team is Wales. She winds her partner up by supporting Wales at rugby, or any team that's playing England. In football, England are only supported if Wales are not involved, which unfortunately is usually the case anyway.

She has a soft spot for the Welsh. She finds them kind and generous and always genial, finding her several Welsh clients easy to get on with, and to chat to. She believes there is an element of truth in the recognisable Welsh stereotypes: the man in the corner of the pub, telling an interesting story before bursting into song; the classic Welsh mam who has her children exactly where she wants them – you wouldn't know it, but she is always in control, while the men spend all their time down the pub. Certainly both her father and grandfather have been known to slip away for a quiet pint or two.

She is proud of her Welsh heritage. She thinks she looks quite Welsh – short, dark haired and stubborn – but she is not in the slightest bit musical, nor does she have any overwhelming urge to live in Wales, given her occupation is unlikely to take her there on a permanent basis.

Yet she has developed an interest in Welsh history, currently reading John Davies's *History of Wales* (even if she did fall asleep reading it the other bedtime!). She wanted to learn another language, and felt it might as well be Welsh: 'It just feels a bit odd, if you identify yourself as partially Welsh, not to be able to speak the language. It seems to be an important characteristic.'

American Pamela Petro emotionally argues that the language is a major factor in the preservation of Welshness whether it be in Wales or across the world: '*Cymru* is a place that only comes into being through speech. I guess you could call it the consequence of language. Wales, by contrast, is a beautiful, wet, green, rocky protrusion that keeps the Irish Sea from breaking upon the Cotswolds. It needs the Welsh language in order to survive, but the language doesn't need it. *Cymru* is a place waiting to be spoken into life at any moment anywhere around the globe, a legion of *terrae incognitae* poised for exploration through speech, music, memory, enthusiasm, and certainly beer.'

Clare doesn't necessarily need the language to work with Welsh clients, but some of her friends are Welsh speaking, including her ex-college boyfriend, and admits it can be useful for gossiping behind people's backs.

She has been trying to learn it for herself in an unstructured way for several years, so Welsh classes at the London Welsh Centre, walking distance from her offices, seemed a natural next step.

And she has found her actions have stimulated interest among her family, particularly the middle sister, who Clare has discovered, also has some pro-Welsh sympathies. The two sisters have had discussions about whether they would be happy to lose Parry, their Welsh surname, if they were to get married. And it has already been agreed that 'Guide Me O Thou Great Redeemer' will be played at Clare's wedding and funeral.

# Heinke

A ONE-TIME MARKET research colleague of mine used to organise what she called 'nice people lunches' to which she would invite only people she liked. Those not invited she considered either too boring or creepy. To be honest I can't actually remember whether I ever received an invite.

I found the custom arrogant and presumptuous. I would hate to think that all my talk of how friendly we Welsh are could feel equally pretentious.

To provide a more unbiased substantiation of our strengths and weaknesses, I will leave the last word to a foreigner.

Heinke Pulhorn is a 40-year-old German who is attending Welsh-language classes at the London Welsh Centre while working as a surgical registrar at the Royal Free Hospital in Hampstead. Until recently she performed a similar function at Morriston Hospital, Swansea, and still has an apartment in the Swansea Uplands, plus a boyfriend in Lampeter to where she retreats at every possible opportunity.

Heinke was born in Frisia, near the Dutch border, but the family moved to her father's birthplace of Bavaria when she was ten. In the mid 1990s she came to London to read for a degree in biological sciences, then returned to Germany to qualify in medicine in the year 2000. She now had a desire to travel, but being 30 she felt it was too late for a gap year, so decided to combine travelling with working. She was really limited to English-speaking countries, so her career has taken her to Crewe, South Africa, Liverpool, and then Morriston.

This was her first exposure to Wales, but unlike some Europeans, she was actually aware of the place. Her home town in Bavaria is twinned with Prestwick in Scotland which she first visited in 1985. The Scots immediately pointed out to her that they were different from the English, adding that there were also the Welsh and the Irish. They claimed that she needn't bother with Wales as it was just like Scotland, only smaller. So her first encounter with the Welsh was going down to Morriston for an interview for a post which she took purely because it was a good job.

Heinke found Britain on the whole to be welcoming to newcomers, but Wales even more so. The Royal Free has a reputation as a particularly friendly hospital, but she feels it is not on the same level as Morriston. Standing at the nurses' desk looking lost on her first day, the ward sister came up to her, asking 'Are you all right, chicken?' This was the same ward sister who Heinke later learnt ran a very tight ship and was as tough as nails, but was still ever so welcoming and friendly. The Welsh patients were also generally far more polite to the staff, showing respect for the doctors as professionals.

Heinke thinks Wales is welcoming and non-threatening. I am a little hesitant when I hear how Llanelli is currently struggling to accommodate the large numbers of Polish immigrants and, watching a recent S4C programme about a trainee probation officer working with druggies, I am reminded of how harsh an environment my home town can be. But I was also made very conscious of the caring nature of the probation officer. And in contrast to Prestwick or South Africa, Heinke in no way found Swansea a dangerous environment in which to live. She feels that migrants, white, black or Asian have been more easily assimilated into the population, and have taken to Welsh culture, even ensuring their children become proficient in the Welsh language.

Her immediate boss in Swansea was English, ex-army, who came to Wales as a registrar. He is now married to a Welsh girl, has four children, all of whom attend a Welsh-language school.

Heinke further observes that 'you can't enter a Welsh house without having cakes shoved at you, and being made to sit in the best chair to have a cup of tea'. This is partly a function of what she sees as its endearing parochialness. When she first worked at Morriston, the hospital had 460 beds. It is now part of a trust incorporating five hospitals and more than 2,000 beds. Yet everybody still knows everybody. It is still really a cottage hospital. The staff know many of the patients, or have had a relative give birth or die in the hospital. Even Cardiff is provincial. You can go to see a rugby match with 70,000 others and are almost guaranteed to meet someone you know.

We are all familiar with the demographic myth that the person sitting next to you on the bus is likely to be related to you six degrees removed. Heinke believes in Wales that there are only three rather than six links in the chain.

But while Wales is a small country where everyone knows everyone, Heinke is also too aware that travelling isn't easy. Morriston Hospital now covers the whole of west Wales as far north as Aberystwyth, and some emergencies across this wide area are even handled in Cardiff. So her job involved a fair amount of travel.

The railways are 'hopelessly inadequate' and while she enjoys driving on the winding country roads, she is also conscious of good roads being few and far between. Heinke recalls hearing a phone-in on the radio when a Welsh motorist warned a traffic reporter that there was an accident at junction 28 on the motorway. 'Which motorway?' asked the reporter. 'The M4 of course' came the reply. There is only one motorway in Wales.

Heinke typically likes to make an effort to integrate into any new environment in which she finds herself. She thus felt the need to understand Welsh place-names better, and to be able to converse on a social level with some of her older patients. So she has worked hard to become fluent in the Welsh language, and now even speaks it with a pronounced west Wales accent.

Being able to speak Welsh helped open doors. A course in Aberystwyth was over-subscribed, leaving Bristol as the closest option. A word in Welsh by the ward sister to the organiser ensured a place was found for her in Aberystwyth. Wales is not unlike Bavaria, suggests Heinke, where some bars won't serve you unless they detect a Bavarian accent.

Heinke also thinks that the presence of many anglicised words in conversations in Welsh, often laughed at by the English, is not a negative but a sign that the language is alive and kicking and keeping up with the times.

When it comes to the English, Heinke recognises that the Welsh have a chip on their shoulder, but it is a feeling with which she can sympathise, and which drew her to the Welsh from the outset. In Liverpool she was always aware of the fact that she wasn't English. She encountered a certain amount of anti-German sentiment, a response which she found to be absent in Wales. And now she is working at the Royal Free, with her acquired Welsh accent, she has become 'the Welsh girl' and is made aware of English prejudices at first hand. On recommending medical procedures learnt in Morriston she is told 'that may be good enough for Wales, but it won't do here'.

She suspects that the English are uncomfortable with the Welsh, a people who have been on these islands far longer than them, and who speak a language they don't understand.

It's easy to make the Welsh laugh and much of the anti-English banter she feels is really in jest. Hospital staff, being trained to show greater respect to patients, were happy to take the advice on board, but 'not if they're English'.

But Heinke still believes there are underlying strong feelings, and sees an essential quality of the Welsh to be their stubbornness, their refusal to accept an English way of life. She understands their nationalism. She thinks it's wonderful that even non-Welsh speakers can belt out 'Hen Wlad Fy Nhadau' without understanding a word of it. And she is conscious of their desire to preserve their friendly provinciality: 'this is the way we are, if you don't like it you can lump it'.

Heinke wanted to do something else that was really Welsh, so she asked to be taken to a rugby match. Never impressed by viewing the game on television, seeing it live in all its physicality, she has become totally hooked.

The game she saw was at Stradey, courtesy of a colleague with a Scarlets season ticket. Six months later, she was also a season ticket holder. And now not only can she discuss playing tactics with an amazing degree of authority, but is privy to all the sporting gossip as she treats many of the team in her capacity as a medical specialist. Her favourite player is definitely Stephen Jones.

A stroke victim from Lampeter had to spend some time in Morriston. The ward sister decided that his visiting son was a Stephen Jones lookalike and the ideal man for Heinke. Unfortunately the old man was discharged before the sister could engineer a meeting. But she did ensure telephone numbers were exchanged, and later, when attending a Welsh-language course in Lampeter, Heinke sent a text to the son suggesting a meeting. They are still an item.

The now boyfriend is a first language Welsh-speaker which must do wonders for Heinke's Welsh. But his Welsh has been learnt not in school but at home. So when asked to help Heinke identify the correct mutation in a particular instance, he replied 'What's a mutation?'

The world of Lampeter is smaller still. Nothing is open on a Sunday evening, not even the petrol station. When her boyfriend's mam read in the media that one recent S4C programme had a zero audience (zero actually meant less than 1,000) she countered by saying she had watched it, and so had her mother, and Mrs Davies next door, so the papers must be wrong.

Heinke, finally, like first generation Englishman Tony Fielden, has fallen in love with the Welsh countryside. She thinks Swansea is 'a dump' but 'it's in such a lovely area'.

American Pamela Petro has argued that the Welsh language can exist as a statement of Welshness anywhere in the world. Wales needs its language, but the language doesn't need Wales. Yet she also adds that 'the desire to learn Welsh is all about place. I can't imagine wanting to learn Welsh without knowing Wales.' And it was in Lampeter that Pamela studied Welsh.

Heinke has not been unhappy in England. She has friends and a good social life. She enjoyed living in Liverpool. The city is vibrant, the Wirral is pretty and Scousers are hilarious.

She enjoyed South Africa, Scotland, Liverpool, but 'it's different this time, and I don't know why. I like the people of course. They'll chat to anybody. And it's smaller: everyone knows each other. It's the old Welsh village thing. But it's the continuous, imposing presence of the country. I feel closer to the land. It's really quite strange. I love the countryside, going for walks, the history, the sights. My feelings are deeper.'

Makes me feel like moving back home.

# Epilogue

**_Cwrs Haf_ Aberystwyth**

# *Cwrs Haf* Aberystwyth

AN HOUR AND a half's lesson each week has not been sufficient to reacquaint my ageing mind with the complexities of the Welsh language. I back away from any attempt at conversation with a Welsh speaker, tongue-tied and forgetful of both grammar and vocabulary. A greater immersion in more continuous conversation has become a necessity.

So off I went in the second week in August 2010 to the Welsh for Adults summer school (*Cwrs Haf*) at Aberystwyth University. The more determined spent a full four weeks on the course; I compromised with just a week's stay. The experience, as well as hopefully improving my language fluency, served almost as a microcosm of these reflections, reminding me of the key elements of being Welsh today, and the differing attitudes that exist among the various segments of the population.

The ludicrously beautiful A44 road from Rhayader to Aberystwyth immediately brought home to me the attractiveness of our homeland. The scenery is stunning, even in comparison with Snowdonia.

It also highlighted how tortuous a journey it is by road through mid Wales, and how isolated Aberystwyth can feel to the traveller. The A44 was reported on TV after a recent accident as the most dangerous road in Wales. This is partly as a result of the terrain, but also how the authorities have not felt the need over the years to develop further the transport infrastructure within the Principality. A fellow student, travelling to the course from Galway in western Ireland, discovered on arriving at Holyhead that the only rail route to Aberystwyth was via Crewe which, not only is in England, a country the other side of Wales from Ireland, but requiring a round trip of about 250 miles, compared to the 100 or so road miles between Holyhead and Aberystwyth.

Another fellow student, an inspector of schools from Pembrokeshire, spoke of the administrative problems currently facing education and health in Wales. I asked him whether the Welsh systems were likely to be exposed to the frightening privatisation threatened by David Cameron's 'Big Society'. He explained no, but added that the population, bombarded as it is by the English-dominated media, are probably ignorant of this fact, reminding me of the remark of Don Anderson, former Labour MP for Swansea East, who thought that devolution for the Welsh people was something of 'a mystery tour'.

The Welsh administration in any case has its own problems, caused possibly by our love of committees. Education in Wales involves 22 separate local authorities and, although the health service has, in contrast, been reduced to seven governing bodies, the number of administrative staff has remained the same, thus failing to achieve any reduction in administrative costs.

The Welsh language however, since my youth in Aberystwyth, has achieved a certain status, and it is now so reassuring on entering Wales to see the bilingual road signs as clear visual proof that you are in a different country – that you are no longer in England. The signposting on the university campus is equally bilingual.

There is still the variation in regional dialect with which to contend. The emphasis of the course was south Wales Welsh (*Fersiwn y De*), although the textbook, which I had first encountered in City Lit in Holborn, was even more specifically entitled *Cwrs Sylfaenol Ceredigion a Gogledd Penfro* (A Basic Course for Cardiganshire and north Pembrokeshire). Our tutor lived in Llandeilo in south Wales, but hailed originally from north Wales, and always provided the alternative north Wales grammar for those in the class who wished to use the north Wales version of the language in classroom conversations.

The various days' topics certainly had a Welsh feel to

them – 'gossiping', 'health', and 'expressing sympathy after a bereavement'.

The welcome was, as ever, friendly, not only for the Welsh learners but for various other groups sharing the campus: foreign students learning English, an Evangelical Church conference (almost every person was carrying a Bible) and a gathering of orthodox Jews. Wales is always glad to welcome the world.

The Evangelicals congregated each day in the Great Hall, the centrepiece of the university's magnificent Arts Centre, which also incorporates a theatre, cinema, two art galleries, various artist and dance studios, a comprehensive bookshop, two restaurants and a bar. All this in a town with a population of just 12,000, in splendid isolation from any other urban development of note. Culture is alive and kicking in mid Wales.

And the Welsh learners and their tutors exhibited all the different characteristics of Welshness I have identified throughout this book. The tutors did their absolute utmost to ensure that all the students conversed in Welsh at all hours of the day and evening, a quite exhausting experience. We all needed a drink by the end of the evening, although the more puritanical of the tutors viewed this with a little disdain. I'd forgotten that the beeriness of the Welsh character has always been countered by a certain narrow-mindedness.

Among the students there were also fluent Welsh speakers attempting to take their understanding of the language and its literature to a higher, even master, level. No longer is Welsh merely a colloquial language only spoken around the hearth.

There were others who now had to learn Welsh for business and administrative reasons. Debbie, a local Aberystwyth nursery assistant, is learning Welsh because her school has switched to being a Welsh-language establishment. Originally from Llangennech, near Llanelli, she, like me, was not encouraged to speak Welsh as a child, and now has non-

Welsh-speaking children, despite an Aberystwyth husband who speaks the language.

Debbie reminded me of many Llanelli people I encountered in my childhood. She was quite happy to have British stamped on her passport; she was not that bothered about learning Welsh, but strongly resented being thought of as not Welsh just because she couldn't speak the language. I feel guilty about not speaking Welsh. She feels it is down to her individual choice and this should not have any bearing on her Welsh nationality.

It slightly worries me that the majority of Welsh learners, encountered in the various classes I have attended, are from the chattering classes or academia. So it is reassuring to learn that the highest proportion of Welsh speakers is to be found among 11- to 16-year-olds who are still at school. And in Welsh-language schools, a majority of these pupils have non-Welsh-speaking parents keen to provide their children with a language lost to their generation.

In Aberystwyth there were several learners like myself merely wanting to make contact with their roots, even if the Welsh language wasn't a significant part of their childhood. Sue, originally from non-Welsh-speaking Tenby, now retired from teaching and living in Berkhampstead, is tempted to move back to Wales. Richard, a 70-year-old from Cardiff, has been attending for five years or more, even though he has yet to advance beyond Level 1. He just loves the company and the Welsh environment. The organisers usually provide him with the same room in the same flat each year. On this occasion, however, they made him switch rooms. So, to ensure he didn't get confused, he posted a photograph of his wife, now sadly deceased, on his bedroom door.

Then there was Brian, an American boy from Pennsylvania with a Welsh mother, on his first holiday outside of America, deciding to learn the language at the same time as visiting the country of his grandmother's birth. It wasn't however his first time outside the United States. He had just returned from a tour of duty in Afghanistan. That sounds even more taxing than Welsh mutations.

There were also foreign immigrants who felt motivated to learn Welsh as part of their assimilation into their new country. This not only included a Polish girl who was setting up in business in Llandysul, but also an American girl, Rebecca, who befriended a fellow musician from Wales, came to Wales to make a CD, and fell in love with the country, the Welsh way of life, and specifically, a Welsh boy.

On the Monday evening, we were all entertained by local harpist, Harriet Earis. Originally from Guildford in Surrey, her love affair with the Celtic harp led her to study for a degree in Celtic Studies, which included mastering all three main Celtic languages. She proved to be not only a fine harpist, of both contemporary and modern music, but a pretty fluent Welsh speaker.

Finally, there was a Japanese girl, Akiko, who was persuaded back in Japan, by a teacher who hailed from Wales, to come to Cardiff to continue her studies in English. She has made many friends here, and now wants to learn our language, just for future holidays with her Welsh friends.

On landing at Heathrow, she was asked by a customs officer how long she planned to stay in England. 'Just for today,' she said, 'I'm merely passing through on my way to Wales.'

The world is becoming aware of Wales even if the English are not.